MUHAMMAD ALI

VISUAL ENCYCLOPEDIA

DK Delhi

Senior Editor Sreshtha Bhattacharya
Editor Neha Ruth Samuel
Art Editors Heena Sharma, Sonali Sharma
Jacket Designer Suhita Dharamjit
Jackets Editorial Coordinator Priyanka Sharma
Senior DTP Designers Neeraj Bhatia, Harish Aggarwal
DTP Designer Sachin Gupta
Picture Researcher Deepak Negi
Managing Jackets Editor Saloni Singh
Picture Research Manager Taiyaba Khatoon
Pre-production Manager Balwant Singh
Production Manager Pankaj Sharma
Managing Editor Kingshuk Ghoshal
Managing Art Editor Govind Mittal

DK London

Project Editor Ashwin Khurana
Senior Art Editor Spencer Holbrook
US Executive Editor Lori Cates Hand
US Editor Ann Barton
Jacket Editor Claire Gell
Jacket Design Development Manager Sophia MTT
Producer, Pre-production Gillian Reid
Senior Producer Angela Graef
Managing Editor Francesca Baines
Managing Art Editor Philip Letsu
Publisher Andrew Macintyre
Art Director Karen Self
Associate Publishing Director Liz Wheeler
Design Director Phil Ormerod
Publishing Director Jonathan Metcalf

Written by Clive Gifford
Consultant: James Buckley Jr.

First American Edition, 2018
Published in the United States by DK Publishing
345 Hudson Street, New York, New York 10014

A WORLD OF IDEAS:
SEE ALL THERE IS TO KNOW

www.dk.com

MUHAMMAD ALI

VISUAL ENCYCLOPEDIA

CONTENTS

1

A STAR IS BORN 6

2

TURNING PRO 24

3

TAKING A STAND 54

READY TO GO

Clay strikes a pose during a 1962 photoshoot in New York City, in the middle of a hectic schedule of fights. He fought and won his fourth contest of the year, a bout against American Billy Daniels, just two days after this photo was taken.

1

A STAR IS BORN

The man we know today as Muhammad Ali was born with the name Cassius Clay. At the tender age of 12, Clay committed his life to boxing. His skill and dedication saw him rise through the ranks of amateur boxing, become a national level amateur champion, and gain an Olympic gold medal—all while he was still a teenager.

GROWING UP

> " THE HOUSE WAS ALWAYS **FULL OF LAUGHTER**... HE ALWAYS HAD SUCH A **HUGE PERSONALITY**. "
>
> *– Rudolph Clay, later known as Rahaman Ali*

Cassius Marcellus Clay Jr. was born in Louisville General Hospital in Kentucky on January 17, 1942. Eighteen months later, along came a younger brother, Rudolph, affectionately known as Rudy.

The brothers played and competed with one another throughout their childhood, with Cassius rarely able to keep still or quiet. They also fought sometimes, wrestling and testing out their strength against each other.

Cassius, though, always wanted to lead and be in charge.

As they grew older, Rudy stayed close to his older brother, following in his footsteps by taking up amateur boxing. He turned professional in 1964, fighting 19 times, and often acted as a sparring partner for his brother.

MEET THE PARENTS

Odessa's **grandfather**, Abe Grady, was said to be a **white Irishman** who emigrated to the United States in the 1870s.

Cassius Clay's parents met when his mother, Odessa, was sixteen. His father, Cassius Clay Sr., worked mostly as a billboard and sign painter and occasionally sold his artworks and painted religious murals, which could be found in churches around Louisville. Odessa sometimes worked as a cook and cleaner for wealthy white families in the city. A deeply religious woman, she made sure her sons were smartly dressed when they attended Baptist church each Sunday.

Cassius was close to his mother, whom he called by her nickname, "Bird." From her, he gained his early beliefs about how to treat people and shared with her his dreams of boxing stardom. Odessa supported her son throughout his boxing career, and attended many of his fights.

LIFE IN LOUISVILLE

To the outside world, the city of Louisville in the state of Kentucky was best known as the location of the Kentucky Derby horse race. In 1947, the Clay family moved into 3302 Grand Avenue—a two-bedroom, single-floor house on the western side of the city.

Cassius Clay and his younger brother Rudy shared a bedroom. They played many games together—from marbles to touch football—although Cassius preferred drawing to team sports. However, he did enjoy playing tricks on his younger brother, such as tying a string to the curtains, which he then pulled at night to pretend there were ghosts in the room.

Cassius and Rudy would sometimes accompany their father on painting jobs, learning how to mix and apply the paint. While their upbringing was mostly comfortable, the family's income wasn't always steady. Many of the brothers' clothes were hand-me-downs from other members of their community or obtained from second-hand stores.

When Cassius **lacked money** for the bus fare, he would run and **race the bus** all the way to school.

> " CASSIUS WAS A VERY **EASY-TO-GET-ALONG-WITH FELLOW**. VERY EASY TO HANDLE. **VERY POLITE.** "
> – *Christine Martin, wife of Joe Martin,*
> *Clay's first boxing coach*

A CHILD AT HEART

On a trip home to Louisville in 1963, Cassius pretends to fight a group of local children outside his family house. Throughout his life, he was fond of children, who in return were charmed by his playfulness and kindness.

A star is born

COUNTER PROTESTS

White supporters of racial segregation gather in 1959 in Little Rock, Arkansas. Two years earlier, mass protests at the enrollment of nine African-American students at Central High School in Little Rock led to troops being sent in to ensure peace was maintained.

RACE MIXING IS ★ ★ COMMUNISM

STO THE RAC MIXIN MARCH O THE HRIS

RACIAL INTEGRATION IN SCHOOLS

A group of young African-American students nervously enter a Tennessee school that had previously been for white people only. In 1954, the US Supreme Court banned segregation in schools. Despite the ban, in practice it still took some years before African-American and white students would be taught together.

RACIAL SEGREGATION

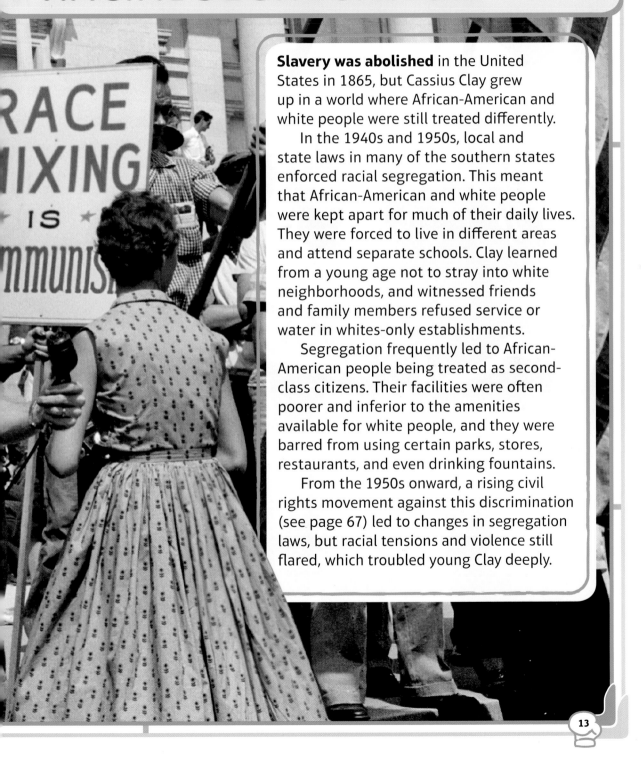

Slavery was abolished in the United States in 1865, but Cassius Clay grew up in a world where African-American and white people were still treated differently.

In the 1940s and 1950s, local and state laws in many of the southern states enforced racial segregation. This meant that African-American and white people were kept apart for much of their daily lives. They were forced to live in different areas and attend separate schools. Clay learned from a young age not to stray into white neighborhoods, and witnessed friends and family members refused service or water in whites-only establishments.

Segregation frequently led to African-American people being treated as second-class citizens. Their facilities were often poorer and inferior to the amenities available for white people, and they were barred from using certain parks, stores, restaurants, and even drinking fountains.

From the 1950s onward, a rising civil rights movement against this discrimination (see page 67) led to changes in segregation laws, but racial tensions and violence still flared, which troubled young Clay deeply.

THE STOLEN SCHWINN

Despite segregation, Louisville was a relatively peaceful city during Cassius Clay's childhood. But a crime committed there would set 12-year-old Clay on the path to greatness. It occurred on the day that he and his friend, John Willis, pedalled across town to visit the Louisville Home Show at the Columbia Auditorium. It gave Clay a chance to enjoy his red-and-white Schwinn bicycle, which had cost his parents $60, a large sum at the time.

After enjoying the show—and especially, the free popcorn—Clay realized his bike had been stolen. Upset and angry, he sought out the nearest policeman, who happened to be in the auditorium's basement. Joe Martin was a white police officer who had coached boxers at the Columbia Gym since 1938. A furious Clay reported the crime, and threatened to find and beat up the thief. Martin calmly suggested that the slender young boy might need to learn how to fight and defend himself first. Clay left without his bike, but with a gym application form that Joe had given him, and a desire to return.

" I TOLD HIM… THAT **IF HE REALLY WANTED TO FIGHT** SOMEONE… COME DOWN AND **BE TAUGHT PROPERLY**. **"**

– Joe Martin

GOOD BALANCE

A 21-year-old Clay enjoys a cycle trip around Louisville, attracting an entourage of neighborhood children excited to see the dashing young boxer. By this time, Clay had moved to Florida, but he returned to his home city whenever he could.

A star is born

15

LEARNING HIS CRAFT

Cassius Clay was entranced by the sounds, sights, and smells of the Columbia Gym and soon became a frequent visitor. On many occasions, his brother Rudy came too.

Joe Martin and the boxers at the gym were not particularly impressed by Clay's talent or his skinny, 89 lb (40 kg) frame, but they soon came to admire his dedication and desire for improvement.

Clay's first amateur bout against a child his own age called Ronnie O'Keefe occurred just six weeks after his first visit to the gym. The two boys flailed away with wild punches over three short, one-minute rounds. Neither boy landed many telling blows, but Clay was declared the winner. He was absolutely thrilled, and was soon heading to the gym as often as possible.

The **1968 World Heavyweight Champion**, Jimmy Ellis, **also trained at the Columbia Gym** alongside young Clay.

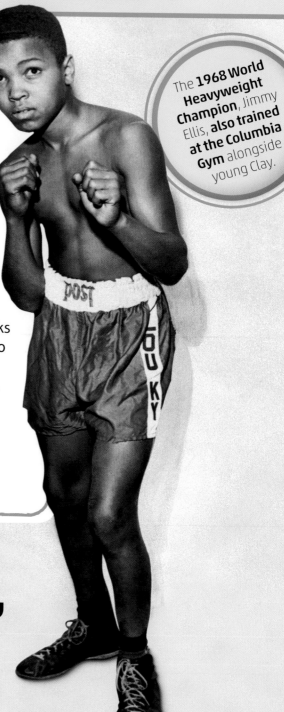

66 ALL HE **EVER WANTED** TO DO WAS **RUN** AND **TRAIN** AND **SPAR**. 99
- Jimmy Ellis

MAKING SACRIFICES

As Cassius Clay's obsession with boxing grew, his days became jam-packed. Many mornings started with a 5 am run across Chickasaw Park before attending school at Central High. There, he would eat huge school lunches to fuel his training, and shadowbox in the school corridors. Clay never used his boxing skills to bully others, although his school principal, Atwood Wilson, sometimes threatened misbehaving students with a visit from him. After school, Clay occasionally worked part-time jobs, but he trained with Joe Martin (pictured here) at the Columbia Gym whenever he could.

Clay also sought out other coaches, and would often be found at a gym at the Grace Community Center, where boxing trainer Fred Stoner helped him improve his technique.

GOLDEN GLOVES

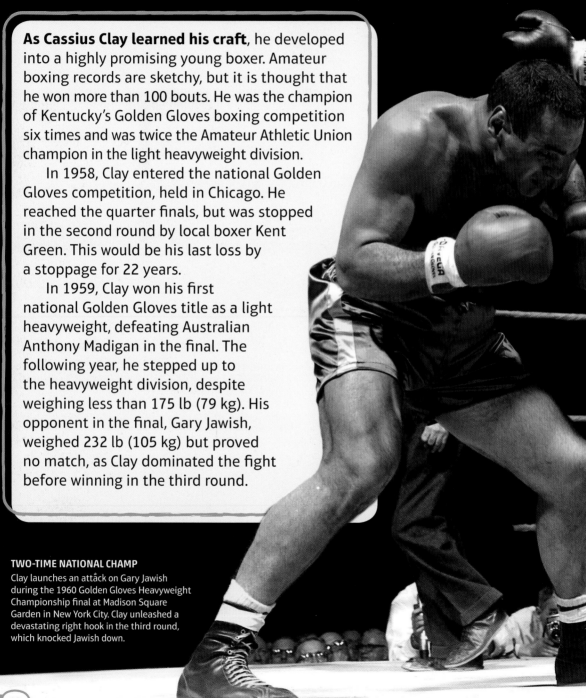

As Cassius Clay learned his craft, he developed into a highly promising young boxer. Amateur boxing records are sketchy, but it is thought that he won more than 100 bouts. He was the champion of Kentucky's Golden Gloves boxing competition six times and was twice the Amateur Athletic Union champion in the light heavyweight division.

In 1958, Clay entered the national Golden Gloves competition, held in Chicago. He reached the quarter finals, but was stopped in the second round by local boxer Kent Green. This would be his last loss by a stoppage for 22 years.

In 1959, Clay won his first national Golden Gloves title as a light heavyweight, defeating Australian Anthony Madigan in the final. The following year, he stepped up to the heavyweight division, despite weighing less than 175 lb (79 kg). His opponent in the final, Gary Jawish, weighed 232 lb (105 kg) but proved no match, as Clay dominated the fight before winning in the third round.

TWO-TIME NATIONAL CHAMP
Clay launches an attack on Gary Jawish during the 1960 Golden Gloves Heavyweight Championship final at Madison Square Garden in New York City. Clay unleashed a devastating right hook in the third round, which knocked Jawish down.

" GOD HAD GIVEN THIS KID **REFLEXES LIKE NO ONE HAD EVER SEEN**. "
– *Bob Surekin, Amateur Athletic Union boxing referee*

A star is born

MAKING THE OLYMPICS

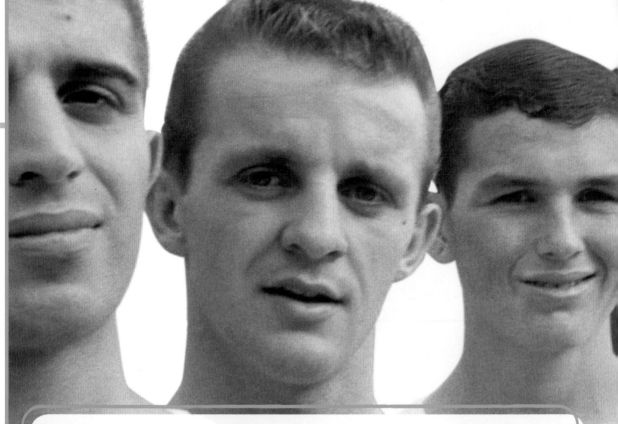

Fresh from his successes at the Golden Gloves, Cassius Clay entered the United States Olympic Amateur Boxing finals in San Francisco, which selected the team for the 1960 Summer Olympics in Rome, Italy. To make the cut, he competed as a light heavyweight and survived a knockdown in the final before ultimately defeating Allen Hudson.

But, there was one more hurdle to overcome—Clay's intense fear of flying. It took hours of reassurance from his old coach, Joe Martin, before he boarded the flight to Italy. Once in Rome, Clay quickly adapted to being in a foreign country for the first time. He enjoyed mixing with other athletes, and even met heavyweight world champion, Floyd Patterson, whom he taunted that he would defeat one day. For all his bravado, though, Clay tended to shy away from partying in favor of preparing for his bouts.

A beaming Clay (far right) leans out from the back of the row of the amateur boxers that formed the US Olympic team. Two members besides Clay—Edward Crook Jr. (fourth from left) and Wilbert "Skeeter" McClure (not pictured here)—would also bring home gold.

TRAINING FOR GOLD

Television journalist Dick Kirschner interviews Clay at the US Olympic boxing team's training camp at Fort Lee, New Jersey, shortly before their trip to Rome. Clay was touted by many experts as the US team's best hope of a boxing gold medal at the Olympics.

Clay **bought a parachute** from an army surplus store **and wore it throughout the flight** to Rome.

A star is born

OLYMPIC GOLD

The confident and brash Cassius Clay came to the Olympic Games in Rome to win, but a line of fighters stood in his way. At just 18 years old, the young Clay had boxing experts divided—could he box as well as he could talk?

Professional boxing matches today consist of up to 12 rounds; before 1982, they could last up to 15 rounds. Olympic boxers are, however, amateurs and so fight a maximum of three rounds.

Clay had to beat three boxers to make it to the final. His extraordinary technique was clear from the outset, when he comfortably defeated the Belgian Yvon Becaus. He continued to impress in the second fight, after which the experienced Soviet Gennadi Shatkov said of the American, "There is no disgrace in losing to a boxer like that." After toppling the tough Australian Anthony Madigan, Clay set up a final against Zbigniew Pietrzykowski from Poland.

The Pole landed some heavy punches in the first two rounds, but Clay found his rhythm in the final round, leaving Pietrzykowski slumped against the ropes. All five judges awarded the fight to Clay on points, earning him the gold medal.

Clay's final opponent **"Zigzy" Pietrzykowski** had been a **bronze medalist** at the 1956 Olympics.

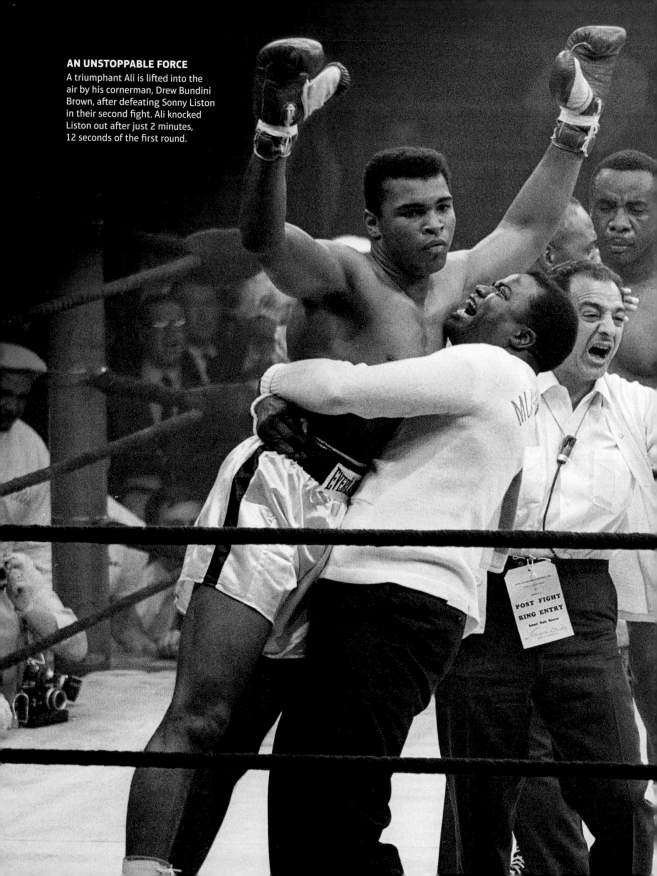

AN UNSTOPPABLE FORCE
A triumphant Ali is lifted into the air by his cornerman, Drew Bundini Brown, after defeating Sonny Liston in their second fight. Ali knocked Liston out after just 2 minutes, 12 seconds of the first round.

2
TURNING PRO

Cassius Clay turned professional in 1960, quickly gaining a reputation for his fast hands and feet. He became the world champion at the age of 22 when he defeated Sonny Liston in 1964. Clay also converted to Islam and changed his name to Muhammad Ali that same year.

Clay bought a **rose-pink Cadillac** with a part of the advance from the **Louisville 11**.

CENTER OF ATTENTION
Clay jokes for the camera during a meeting with nine of the Louisville 11 in early 1963. He holds up six fingers to predict he will defeat his next opponent, Douglas Jones, in the sixth round.

THE LOUISVILLE 11

Cassius Clay returned home in triumph after the Olympic Games. A large crowd greeted him at Louisville's airport and a 25-vehicle convoy transported him to a hero's welcome at his old high school. Offers to manage Clay as he turned professional flooded in, from Rocky Marciano, Joe Martin, and Cus D'Amato (Floyd Patterson's manager), among others.

Because hiring a manager and trainer was expensive, Clay signed a contract with the Louisville Sponsoring Group, or the Louisville 11—a collection of 11 wealthy businessmen, most of whom were from Clay's hometown. As well as paying for Clay's training expenses, this group paid Clay a large advance of $10,000, and guaranteed his income for the first two years of his professional career. In return, Clay would have to share 50 percent of the prize money from each fight with them.

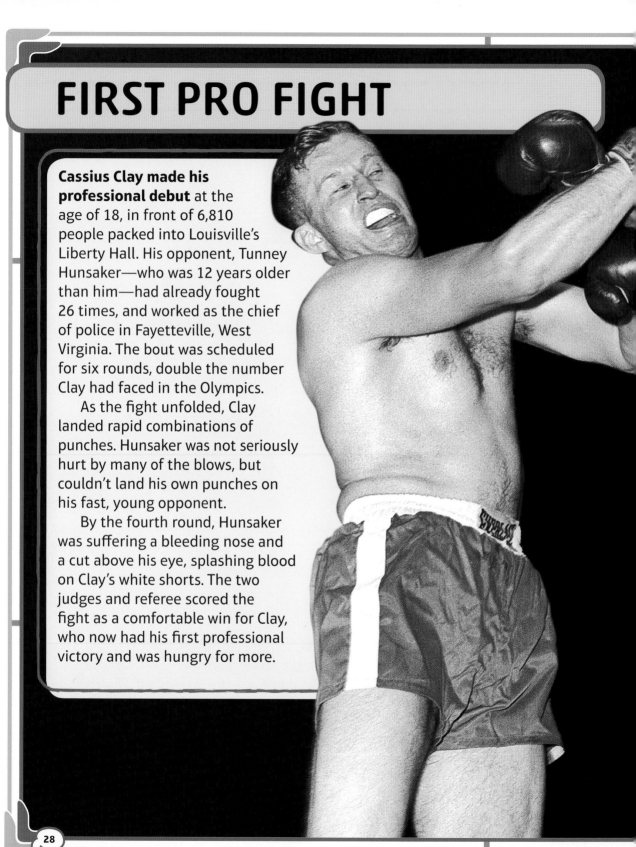

FIRST PRO FIGHT

Cassius Clay made his professional debut at the age of 18, in front of 6,810 people packed into Louisville's Liberty Hall. His opponent, Tunney Hunsaker—who was 12 years older than him—had already fought 26 times, and worked as the chief of police in Fayetteville, West Virginia. The bout was scheduled for six rounds, double the number Clay had faced in the Olympics.

As the fight unfolded, Clay landed rapid combinations of punches. Hunsaker was not seriously hurt by many of the blows, but couldn't land his own punches on his fast, young opponent.

By the fourth round, Hunsaker was suffering a bleeding nose and a cut above his eye, splashing blood on Clay's white shorts. The two judges and referee scored the fight as a comfortable win for Clay, who now had his first professional victory and was hungry for more.

> **" HE'S AWFULLY GOOD FOR AN 18-YEAR-OLD AND AS FAST AS A MIDDLEWEIGHT. "**
> – *Tunney Hunsaker, about Clay after the fight*

The money from the **ticket sales** for the Hunsaker fight was **donated** to a local **children's hospital**.

FIGHT FILE

OPPONENT: Tunney Hunsaker, age 30, American

DATE AND PLACE: October 29, 1960, Freedom Hall, Louisville, Kentucky

RESULT: Clay won by unanimous decision (6th round)

Turning pro

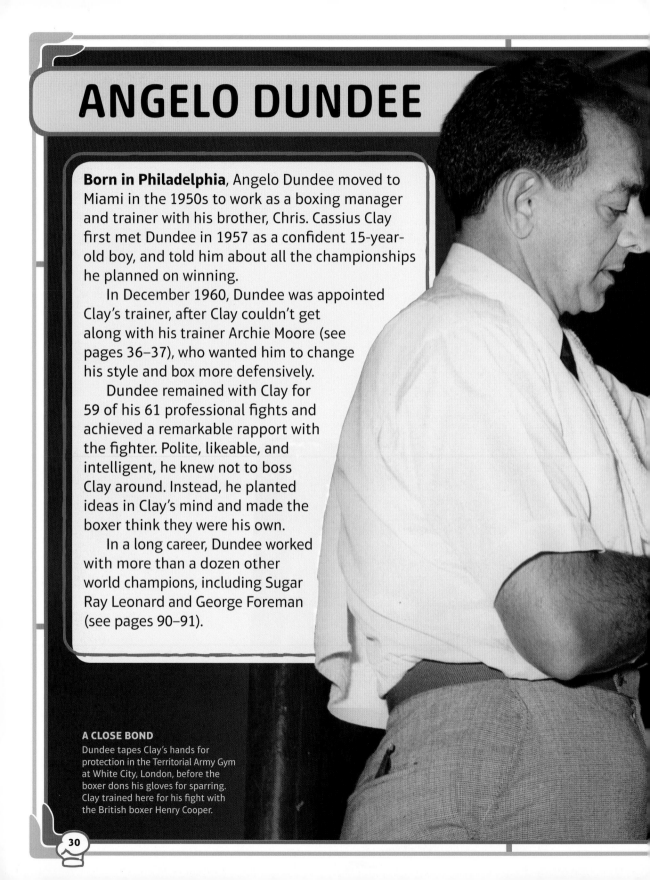

ANGELO DUNDEE

Born in Philadelphia, Angelo Dundee moved to Miami in the 1950s to work as a boxing manager and trainer with his brother, Chris. Cassius Clay first met Dundee in 1957 as a confident 15-year-old boy, and told him about all the championships he planned on winning.

In December 1960, Dundee was appointed Clay's trainer, after Clay couldn't get along with his trainer Archie Moore (see pages 36–37), who wanted him to change his style and box more defensively.

Dundee remained with Clay for 59 of his 61 professional fights and achieved a remarkable rapport with the fighter. Polite, likeable, and intelligent, he knew not to boss Clay around. Instead, he planted ideas in Clay's mind and made the boxer think they were his own.

In a long career, Dundee worked with more than a dozen other world champions, including Sugar Ray Leonard and George Foreman (see pages 90–91).

A CLOSE BOND
Dundee tapes Clay's hands for protection in the Territorial Army Gym at White City, London, before the boxer dons his gloves for sparring. Clay trained here for his fight with the British boxer Henry Cooper.

" IF ANGELO HADN'T BEEN IN MY CORNER, I WOULDN'T BE WHERE I AM TODAY. "

– Muhammad Ali in a New York Times interview in 1981

Dundee also **trained the boxer Jimmy Ellis** and **was in his corner** rather than Ali's when the pair fought in 1971.

5TH STREET GYM

Located in a run-down part of Miami Beach, the 5th Street Gym was opened in 1950 by boxing promoter Chris Dundee, with his younger brother, Angelo, operating as a trainer. Reached by a rickety flight of stairs, this gym was a no-frills place of work with just the bare essentials for boxing, including training equipment and rubdown tables where boxers could have their tired bodies massaged.

Cassius Clay threw himself into training at the 5th Street Gym as soon as he arrived in Florida in 1960. It would remain his prime training base throughout the rest of the decade. There, he spent long sessions with Angelo Dundee (see pages 30–31) and watched other boxers while resting, especially enjoying the slick skills of Cuban welterweight, Luis Manuel Rodríguez—who would become world champion in 1963.

Thousands of fighters and spectators passed through this celebrated gym, often called the "University of Boxing," before its closure in 1992.

> ❝TRAINING HIM WAS A WHOLE DIFFERENT BALLGAME FROM MOST FIGHTERS. YOU DIDN'T HAVE TO PUSH. IT WAS LIKE JET PROPULSION. JUST TOUCH HIM AND HE TOOK OFF.❞
> – Angelo Dundee

BUILDING A REPUTATION

Cassius Clay lurches away from a powerful right-hand punch thrown by his opponent George Logan in April, 1962. It was Clay's 13th professional fight in the middle of a hectic period, which saw him fight and win 13 bouts in just 17 months.

The first fight came within ten days of Clay's arrival in Miami in December, 1960. During this period, his boxing education continued in the ring against a variety of opponents, and out of the ring with Angelo Dundee, who taught Clay everything he knew about defense, preparation, and tactics.

In 1961, Clay enjoyed his first professional knockout in his fourth fight, when he beat Jimmy Robinson just 94 seconds into the first round. In the same year, he defeated the 6-ft, 7-in (2-m) giant Duke Sabedong. In his 11th fight, Clay recovered from his first professional knockdown to defeat Sonny Banks in four rounds.

In each bout, Clay found a way to win and, along the way, he sealed his status as heavyweight boxing's fastest rising star.

FIGHT FILE

 OPPONENT: George Logan, age 25, American

 DATE AND PLACE: April 23, 1962, Sports Arena, Los Angeles, California

 RESULT: Clay won by technical knockout (4th round)

INGEMAR JOHANSSON

Clay helps Swedish heavyweight boxer Ingemar Johansson with his protective headgear. Clay sparred with this former world champion in Miami in 1961, but only for two rounds. Johansson's trainer stopped this session because Clay's swift hands and feet were making Johansson look foolish.

" IF YOU DON'T BREAK SOME RECORDS YOU'RE A NO ONE. I WANT TO BREAK BOXING RECORDS... TO BE THE **YOUNGEST HEAVYWEIGHT CHAMPION IN HISTORY.** "

– *Cassius Clay in* Sports Illustrated *magazine, October 1961*

Turning pro

DEFEATING THE OLD MONGOOSE

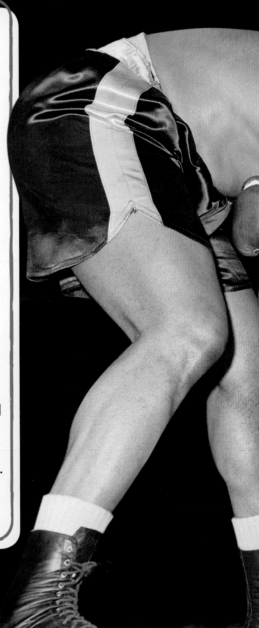

Known as "The Old Mongoose," boxer Archie Moore had turned professional seven years before Cassius Clay was born, and had won more than 180 bouts in his career. Moore had even been Clay's trainer for a short while, in 1960.

By the time he faced Clay, though, Moore was in his mid-forties. He was no match for Clay's rapid-fire punching and lightning fast footwork.

Before the fight, Clay predicted that, "Moore will fall in four," while Moore had responded that he had invented a new punch called the "lip buttoner," which would silence Clay. The verbal sparring between the pair helped sell out the 16,200 capacity Sports Arena, the Californian venue for the spectacle.

In the fight, it was clear that Moore's methodical defense could not keep Clay's punches at bay. The referee nearly stopped the fight in the third round, but finally stepped in during the fourth after Moore suffered his third knockdown of the round.

Clay was triumphant. Moore fought just once more in 1963, before retiring.

Archie Moore was the undisputed **light heavyweight world champion** from **1952** to **1960**.

" CASSIUS PROVED THAT **HE WAS EVERYTHING I THOUGHT HE WASN'T**. I HAD HOPED TO STAY CLOSE TO HIM, WEAR HIM DOWN, BUT IT DIDN'T WORK. "
– *Archie Moore*

Turning pro

THE LOUISVILLE LIP

Cassius Clay had always possessed a quick wit, but as his professional career took off, he began to excel in prefight predictions, jokes, and jibes. This earned him the nickname, the "Louisville Lip".

He was inspired, in part, by the famous wrestler, "Gorgeous" George Wagner, who played the boastful villain before and during his bouts, attracting large crowds. Clay followed a similar path, bragging outrageously about his own talents and declaring himself "The Greatest" long before he had even fought for a world championship. He began dismissing his opponents as "ugly" or mocked them with his scathing poems.

Far from discouraging him, Clay's trainer, Angelo Dundee, enjoyed the boxer's antics as they increased media and public interest in the young fighter. "Trash talking" was not common in this era, and few sports people of the time were as funny or provocative as the "Louisville Lip".

> " I SAW **FIFTEEN THOUSAND PEOPLE** COMING TO SEE THIS MAN GET BEAT AND **HIS TALKING DID IT**. I SAID, THIS IS A GOOD IDEA! "
> – *Cassius Clay talking about wrestler, "Gorgeous" George*

MEDIA ATTENTION

Ever alert for a photo opportunity that would make the newspapers, Clay sits pretending to study a paper on psychological warfare before his fight with Sonny Liston. He is flanked by his trainer, Angelo Dundee (left), and cornerman Drew Bundini Brown, who both would frequently participate in his stunts.

COOPER IN FIVE
Clay displays five fingers, the number of rounds he predicts his 1963 fight with Henry Cooper will last. He told reporters, "It ain't no jive, Henry Cooper will go in five!". This was one of the many prefight predictions he made correctly between 1961 and 1963.

FIGHT OF THE YEAR

Cassius Clay's second fight of 1963 saw him fill up New York City's famous Madison Square Garden. Many of the 18,732 spectators came to support Clay's hometown opponent, Douglas Jones, hoping to see the "Louisville Lip" fail.

Clay predicted he would knock Jones out in six rounds, but when the two clashed in the media, he revised his forecast to four rounds.

In the early rounds, Clay was surprisingly meek, and a powerful right-hand punch from Jones during the first round stopped Clay in his tracks. Clay fought hard to regain control of the fight in the middle rounds, but was jeered as the fourth round passed and his prediction failed. It would take a late flurry of punches in the final two rounds of the ten-round contest for Clay to secure a narrow points victory.

One of the oldest American boxing magazines, *The Ring*, labelled the bout, the "Fight of the Year," but many thought Clay was lucky to prevail and needed to improve greatly if he hoped for a shot at becoming the world champion.

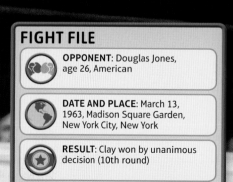

FIGHT FILE

OPPONENT: Douglas Jones, age 26, American

DATE AND PLACE: March 13, 1963, Madison Square Garden, New York City, New York

RESULT: Clay won by unanimous decision (10th round)

DREW BUNDINI BROWN

Trainer and cornerman, Drew Bundini Brown was part of boxer Sugar Ray Robinson's entourage before joining Cassius Clay's camp in 1963.

Growing up, the Florida-born Brown had lived a colorful life. He had lied about his age to join the United States Navy at age 13. Discharged two years later, he spent the next 12 years traveling the world as a sailor on merchant ships.

After joining forces with Clay, Brown quickly made himself indispensable as a fast-talking joker, sidekick, and cheerleader for the champ-in-waiting. He also coined one of Clay's most famous phrases, "float like a butterfly, sting like a bee."

Except for a short spell from 1965 to 1967, when he was ousted from Clay's entourage by the Nation of Islam (see page 50), Brown remained in Clay's corner to the end of the boxer's career.

SUPPORTING THE CHAMP
Clay and Brown ride around Miami in February 1964, days before Clay's world title fight against Sonny Liston. Brown helped motivate Clay and became a key member of his training camp on fight nights.

CLAY, THE RECORDING ARTIST

THE SINGING BOXER
Clay sings a track for his debut record at the Columbia Records 30th Street studio in New York City. His album, *I Am The Greatest*, was a surprise success when it came out in 1963.

Cassius Clay's debut album *I Am The Greatest* was released in 1963. It contained mostly spoken word poems written by Clay in partnership with comedy writer Gary Belkin.

Some of the poems on the album, such as *Will The Real Sonny Liston Please Fall Down*, poked fun at the world heavyweight champion Clay hoped to fight and defeat the following year. Also included were Clay's version of *Stand By Me*, the Ben E. King hit, and *The Gang's All Here*, with Clay's musical idol, Sam Cooke, singing backing vocals.

The album gained Clay a 1964 Grammy nomination for best comedy performance. Clay followed up on this musical venture in 1976, when he recorded a children's album called *The Adventures of Ali and His Gang vs. Mr. Tooth Decay*.

FIGHT FILE

OPPONENT: Henry Cooper, age 28, British

DATE AND PLACE: June 18, 1963, Wembley Stadium, London, UK

RESULT: Clay won by technical knockout (5th round)

"YOU GOT A QUEEN, YOU NEED A KING. **I AM KING! "**
– *Cassius Clay at the weigh-in for the fight*

THE UNSEEN
Clay strikes Cooper with a low blow, which the referee fails to spot during the fight. A low blow is any punch below an imaginary line drawn from the hip bones across the body.

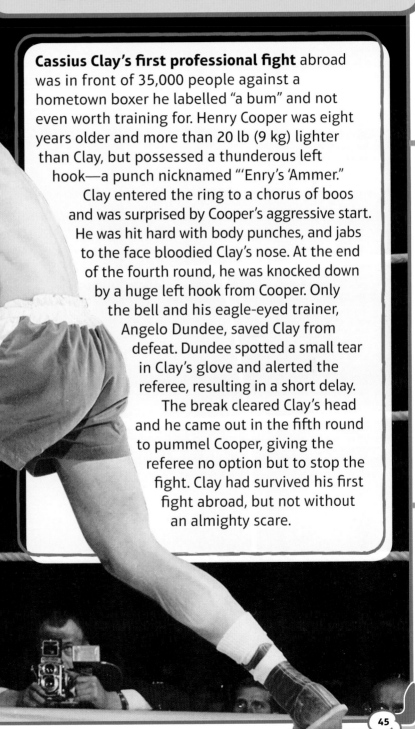

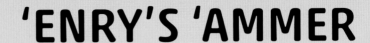

Cassius Clay's first professional fight abroad was in front of 35,000 people against a hometown boxer he labelled "a bum" and not even worth training for. Henry Cooper was eight years older and more than 20 lb (9 kg) lighter than Clay, but possessed a thunderous left hook—a punch nicknamed "'Enry's 'Ammer." Clay entered the ring to a chorus of boos and was surprised by Cooper's aggressive start. He was hit hard with body punches, and jabs to the face bloodied Clay's nose. At the end of the fourth round, he was knocked down by a huge left hook from Cooper. Only the bell and his eagle-eyed trainer, Angelo Dundee, saved Clay from defeat. Dundee spotted a small tear in Clay's glove and alerted the referee, resulting in a short delay. The break cleared Clay's head and he came out in the fifth round to pummel Cooper, giving the referee no option but to stop the fight. Clay had survived his first fight abroad, but not without an almighty scare.

HOWARD BINGHAM

The young photographer Howard Bingham was just starting out at the *Los Angeles Sentinel* newspaper when he first met Cassius Clay and his brother Rudy. It was April 1962, just days before Cassius's fight with George Logan. The Clay brothers were new to the city, so Bingham offered to show them around in his old Dodge Dart car. It would be the start of a lifelong friendship between Clay and Bingham.

The pair, who shared the same sense of humor, traveled the world together. Bingham took more than half a million photographs of Clay, as well as covering many other news and sports events.

A modest and community-minded person, Bingham lived in the same small house in Los Angeles for most of his life. He died at the age of 77, in 2016, just five months after Ali.

❝ I HAVE THE **BEST FRIEND IN THE WORLD**... HE'S ALWAYS THERE WHEN SOMEONE NEEDS HIM. **THERE'S NO ONE LIKE HIM.** ❞

– *Muhammad Ali on Howard Bingham*

Turning pro

RICHES AND REWARDS

By **March 1964**, three years into his professional career, Cassius Clay had earned one million dollars.

For his second professional bout in 1960 he had received $200, but as he continued to win in the ring, his reputation began to grow—and so did his prize money. He received more than $56,000 to fight Henry Cooper in 1963 and more than $450,000 for his February 1964 bout against Sonny Liston—at a time when the average wage in the United States was $88 per week.

While much of the money went to training expenses and the share of the Louisville Sponsoring Group (see pages 26–27), Clay still got to enjoy some of the rewards, such as buying a new home for his parents in Louisville.

BIG MONEY
Clay poses with what was supposed to represent a million dollars in the Bank of America vaults in Los Angeles. This image became one of 40 *Sports Illustrated* magazine covers to feature Clay.

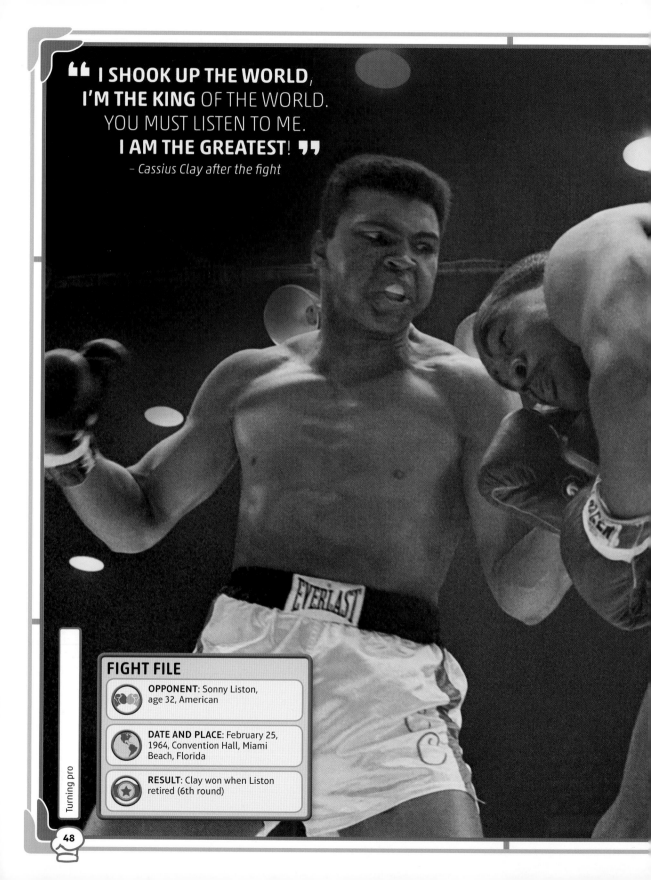

> " I SHOOK UP THE WORLD,
> I'M THE KING OF THE WORLD.
> YOU MUST LISTEN TO ME.
> I AM THE GREATEST! "
> – *Cassius Clay after the fight*

FIGHT FILE

OPPONENT: Sonny Liston, age 32, American

DATE AND PLACE: February 25, 1964, Convention Hall, Miami Beach, Florida

RESULT: Clay won when Liston retired (6th round)

Cassius Clay's first attempt at a world title was his 1964 fight against Sonny Liston. In the build-up to the bout, Clay provoked and upset the reigning champion with stunts and taunts, including calling Liston a "big, ugly bear."

Despite his bravado, Clay feared the hard-hitting Liston and entered the fight as an underdog. After all, in his previous two fights (both against Floyd Patterson) Liston had demolished his opponent with knockouts in the first round.

Liston charged at Clay from the start, but found his challenger's movements too fast to land many powerful punches. Clay boxed sharply and had taken control by the third round.

Disaster struck Clay in round four, when his eyes began stinging and his vision blurred. He nearly quit, but urged on by his coach Angelo Dundee, survived the next round and attacked Liston heavily in the sixth. Liston, his face bruised and his shoulder injured, didn't come out for round seven. In one of boxing's biggest shocks, Clay was now heavyweight champion of the world.

NATION OF ISLAM

Islam is a religion with more than 1.6 billion followers. Beginning in the 7th century in modern-day Saudi Arabia, the faith spread quickly. Today, Islam is practiced globally.

The Nation of Islam (NOI), however, is different. It was founded in Detroit, Michigan, by Wallace D. Fard in 1930. Four years later, Elijah Muhammad became its leader. The NOI shared many beliefs and practices with Islam, such as praying five times a day. However, the group also promoted other ideas, such as the African-American community relying on itself for work. It also proposed that African-Americans and white people live separately, in opposition to the teachings of the civil rights leader Martin Luther King Jr. (see page 67), who believed in ending segregation.

As a young man, Cassius Clay identified with the NOI and its beliefs, and at one point, he was the group's most recognizable figure.

ELIJAH MUHAMMAD
Clay meets NOI leader Elijah Muhammad (right). In the period of Elijah Muhammad's leadership, membership of the NOI rose from 400 in 1952 to more than 200,000 by the end of the 1960s.

MALCOLM X

When introduced, Malcolm X did **not know** that Cassius Clay was a **famous boxer**.

Born in Omaha, Nebraska, Malcolm Little did not become Malcolm X until 1950. He changed his name to "X" in order to be free of the surname, which would have been that of a slave master.

Confident and charismatic, Malcolm X became a fearless spokesperson for the Nation of Islam (NOI) in the 1950s. He inspired Cassius Clay—and his younger brother Rudy—to join the NOI, which was considered a controversial group.

In 1964, Malcolm X left the NOI, but he remained a devout Muslim and civil rights activist until he was killed in 1965.

A SHOULDER TO LEAN ON
In 1964, Clay fans were jubilant after the boxer defeated Sonny Liston to win his first world heavyweight title. With the excited crowd around him, Malcolm X (right) rests a friendly arm on the new boxing champion.

Turning pro

> **" I AM MUHAMMAD ALI**, A **FREE NAME**—IT MEANS BELOVED OF GOD, AND **I INSIST PEOPLE USE IT** WHEN PEOPLE SPEAK TO ME. **"**
> – Muhammad Ali announcing his change of name to the world in March 1964

A NEW JOURNEY
Muhammad Ali shakes the hand of Nation of Islam leader Elijah Muhammad (right) when visiting his Chicago home in 1966. Ali considered Elijah Muhammad his foremost guide to Islam.

CLAY BECOMES ALI

By defeating Sonny Liston to become the heavyweight champion, Cassius Clay made the entire boxing world sit up and take notice of him. His next move, though, would make news beyond the world of boxing.

Clay had sought a faith to guide him through the turbulent times of the 1960s in the United States. Having attended many meetings of the Nation of Islam (NOI), and influenced by the African-American leader Malcolm X, Clay converted to Islam. Soon after the Liston fight, he told reporters that he had changed his name to Cassius X because "Clay" was his unwanted slave name. Less than two weeks later, NOI leader Elijah Muhammad announced that Cassius Clay would now be called Muhammad Ali.

Some people were angry and fearful of the young champion's change of name and religion. Most newspapers continued to refer to him as Cassius Clay for years afterward, and certain venues refused to stage his fights.

During this time, Clay—now known as Muhammad Ali—sought support from the NOI. In 1967, Herbert Muhammad—one of Elijah Muhammad's sons—took over from the Louisville Sponsoring Group (see pages 26–27) to become Ali's manager.

SUNDAY NEWS

PROBE ERNIE DEATH THEO

30,000 MA
IN VIET PRO

TAKING A STAND

The 1960s was a period of great change in both American society and world politics. Muhammad Ali took a courageous stand against the Vietnam War, resulting in a three-year ban from boxing. During this time, Ali went on a lecture tour of colleges.

SWEET AND SOUR

After fighting abroad earlier in 1966, Muhammad Ali returned to the United States to take on the hard-punching Cleveland Williams, nicknamed "Big Cat." It would be Ali who pulled out a performance that left boxing experts purring.

In less than three highly destructive rounds, Ali reeled off more than 100 punches while barely being hit himself. He knocked Williams down four times and dazzled the 35,460-strong crowd at the Houston Astrodome with an utterly dominant performance.

However, things turned sour in Ali's next fight. He was angered by his opponent Ernie Terrell calling him "Clay"—Ali's former name—before the fight. After gaining control of the fight in the middle rounds, Ali inflicted a brutal beating on Terrell.

Ali was unable to knock Terrell out, but pummelled him, shouting, "What's my name?" in between blows. Ali won the fight, though many ringside observers felt it was an ugly victory.

" THAT NIGHT, HE WAS THE MOST DEVASTATING FIGHTER WHO EVER LIVED. "

– Howard Cosell, about Ali's bout against Williams

KNOCKED OUT

Ali walks away after knocking down Cleveland Williams at the end of round two. This was the third of four knockdowns that Williams suffered at Ali's hands in this bout.

FIGHT FILE

OPPONENT: Cleveland Williams, age 33, American

DATE AND PLACE: November 14, 1966, Houston Astrodome, Houston, Texas

RESULT: Ali won by technical knockout (3rd round)

Taking a stand

THE VIETNAM WAR

In 1954, the southeast Asian country of Vietnam gained its independence from France. Vietnam was split into two—a northern half controlled by communist forces and a southern part that counted the United States among its allies.

When North Vietnam attacked South Vietnam, American leaders were fearful of the spread of communism. In the following years, the United States increased its military aid to South Vietnam—from less than 1,000 military advisors in 1960 to more than 485,600 troops in 1967. They hoped to use their technological superiority to secure a rapid victory.

However, American troops found themselves fighting an often hidden enemy who relied on hit-and-run raids, ambushes, and acts of sabotage. Progress was slow, and casualties—both military and civilian—mounted until 1973, when US forces withdrew.

In 1975, North Vietnamese armies gained control of South Vietnam and the country was reunified as one nation the following year.

BOOTS ON THE GROUND
Troops from the 101st Airborne Division are deployed on the ground from a helicopter northwest of the town of Dak To in South Vietnam. This US Army division suffered almost 20,000 deaths or injuries during the Vietnam War.

Taking a stand

" WE ARE **FIGHTING A WAR**
WITH NO FRONT LINES...
THE **ENEMY HIDES IN** THE
JUNGLES AND MOUNTAINS. "
– General William C. Westmoreland,
Commander of the United States forces
in Vietnam, 1967

ALI REFUSES THE DRAFT

Starting in the 1950s, the United States became involved in the conflict in Vietnam (see pages 58–59). Later, American military required healthy young men to enlist in the army—this was known as the draft. Muhammad Ali refused to be inducted, arguing that as a Muslim he adhered to the non-violent principles of Islam. He fervently believed that the United States should not be fighting in Vietnam.

As a result, the courts fined Ali $10,000, confiscated his passport, and sentenced him to five years in prison. Although Ali appealed the conviction and he remained free, he was banned from boxing for the next three years. Boxing authorities were also angered at Ali's stance and stripped him of his heavyweight title.

Through all of this, he always stood by his beliefs. While many people viewed Ali as unpatriotic, others thought he was a hero for speaking out against the war.

MARCHING IN PROTEST

In 1968, Ali made a rousing speech in San Francisco to a crowd of 12,500 people protesting against the Vietnam War draft. The large crowd adored the boxer. Here, an activist hands him a bouquet of flowers.

> **"** I AIN'T GOT **NO QUARREL** WITH THEM **VIETCONG**. **"**
> – *Muhammad Ali, 1967*

THE TRIAL IN TEXAS

Ali talks to reporters on his way to court in Houston, Texas in June 1967. It took the jury just 20 minutes to dismiss Ali's claim that he was a "conscientious objector" because of his religious beliefs. *Time* magazine wrote, "it appears unlikely that Clay… will ever again be a championship contender."

Taking a stand

HOWARD COSELL

Born in North Carolina, Howard Cosell studied law at New York University. After serving in the United States Army during World War II, he continued his legal career, while also working for a New York radio show about baseball between 1953 and 1956.

Turning to sports broadcasting full-time, Cosell's flamboyant style and in-depth commentary were more typical of serious news reporting than sports. He became a household name, greatly influencing sports journalism in American television.

Despite their different personalities and backgrounds, Cosell and Muhammad Ali hit it off, and together possessed great on-screen chemistry. They shared many memorable exchanges on television, often comic and sometimes argumentative.

The pair had great respect for each other. Cosell also supported calls for Ali's return to boxing when the boxer was banned (see pages 60–61). After Cosell's death in 1995, he was included in the International Boxing Hall of Fame to honor his contribution to the sport.

"YOU'RE A PHONY, AND THAT **THING ON YOUR HEAD** COMES FROM **THE TAIL OF A PONY.** **"**

– Muhammad Ali's witty reply about Cosell's wig during a 1974 interview

> **"** I'M EXPECTED TO GO... **FREE PEOPLE IN SOUTH VIETNAM,** AND AT THE SAME TIME **MY PEOPLE HERE ARE GETTING BRUTALIZED...** **"**
> – *Muhammad Ali, speaking during one of his lectures*

INSPIRING THE YOUTH
Ali speaks at St. John's University in New York City. He included jokes and his own poems in his talks, often ending with the rhyme, "I like your school and admire your style, but your pay is so small, I won't be back for a while."

SPEAKING OUT

After Muhammad Ali was found guilty of refusing the draft in June 1967, his life was turned upside down. He could not leave the United States or box anywhere within its borders. Many public figures spoke out against him, and his legal appeals against the court's decision would take nearly four years.

It was a deeply unsettling time for Ali—he was deprived of his main source of income and to make matters worse, did not know if he would be sent to prison or be able to box professionally ever again.

While Ali continued to train and study Islam, he also spent much of this period talking to college students all over the country. Ali spent weeks drafting speeches that he gave to more than 200 colleges, for which he was paid. Ali spoke about his opposition to the Vietnam War, his faith, and issues such as segregation and black pride. It enabled him to reach new audiences, not just boxing fans.

THE PEOPLE'S CHAMP

Ali greets students of St. John's University after giving a talk there in 1971. Despite frequent hecklers and opposition among the audiences, Ali was often heartened by the warm reception he received, especially on issues such as his stance on the Vietnam War.

Taking a stand

PROTESTING THE WAR

Some Americans opposed the Vietnam War (see pages 58–59) from the start, but as the conflict raged on, the numbers of anti-war protestors swelled.

As the hope of the United States military gaining a quick victory dissolved and casualties mounted, more Americans began to question and oppose their country's involvement in the war. In 1968 alone, more than 16,000 American personnel lost their lives in Vietnam, and around 58,000 during the entire war.

The following year saw many large anti-war demonstrations across the country. There were also pro-war rallies held around the country, as the issue divided American society.

ANTI-WAR SENTIMENT
On November 15, 1969, anti-war protestors march down Pennsylvania Avenue in Washington, D.C. This rally featured close to half a million people. A mostly peaceful protest, it was the largest, single anti-war demonstration in American history.

Taking a stand

MARTIN LUTHER KING JR.

Born in Atlanta in 1929, Martin Luther King Jr. followed in his father's footsteps to become a Baptist minister. Inspired by the Indian political leader Mahatma Gandhi's use of non-violent resistance, King was at the forefront of the American Civil Rights movement in the 1950s and 1960s.

King preached protest and change without violence in the form of peaceful marches, strikes, and the boycott of services. He opposed segregation (see pages 12–13) in all walks of life and became a critic of the Vietnam War (see pages 58–59).

King won the Nobel Peace Prize in 1964, the same year that then US president Lyndon B. Johnson signed the Civil Rights Act. This act created equal rights for all people in areas such as voting and education.

In 1968, while supporting a strike by African-American sanitation workers in Memphis, Tennessee, King was assassinated.

THE MARCH ON WASHINGTON
King addresses more than 250,000 protestors who had gathered in Washington, D.C. in 1963. His powerful speech—hoping for a future where his children would be judged by their characters, not the color of their skin—resonated all around the world.

ALI, THE FATHER

Muhammad Ali's years in exile from boxing saw great changes in his personal life. In 1967, Ali married Khalilah (formerly known as Belinda Tolona Boyd), and soon after became a father for the first time.

The couple had first met in 1961 when Ali had visited her school, the University of Islam, in Chicago. They married in August 1967, and moved from Chicago to Philadelphia, before settling in New Jersey in 1971.

Ali loved children and was overjoyed when their first child, Maryum (known as May May), was born in 1968. Two years later, the couple greeted the arrival of twin daughters Jamillah and Rasheda. They also had a son, Muhammad Eban, two years after Ali's boxing ban was lifted.

With his third wife, Veronica Porsche, Ali would have two more children— Hana and Laila (see page 110). Later in life, Ali adopted a boy, Asaad, with his fourth wife, Lonnie (see pages 106–107).

❝ HE MADE ME FEEL LIKE **THE MOST SPECIAL GIRL** IN THE WORLD... **EVERY LITTLE SCRIBBLE** I DID, **HE KEPT IT IN A BOX**. **❞**
– *Maryum Ali*

FATHER AND SON
Ali kisses his newborn son, Muhammad Eban Ali Jr., alongside his wife Khalilah. Ali's first son was born on May 14, 1972—just 13 days after Ali defeated Canadian boxer, George Chuvalo.

THE TIDE TURNS

Muhammad Ali's mid-to-late twenties should have been the peak of his boxing career, but instead he was barred from the sport for more than three and a half years.

By the end of the 1960s, though, people's attitudes toward the Vietnam War had begun to change. As more people turned against the war, Ali's principles and his stand against the conflict no longer seemed as dangerous and unpatriotic as before. He received increasing support from public figures and, while his legal appeals dragged on, attempts were made to get him back into the boxing ring.

In 1970, the city of Atlanta, Georgia, finally granted Ali a license to box, after more than 20 other states had refused to do so. Ali returned to a strict training regime and fought an exhibition bout, before taking on Jerry Quarry in Atlanta on October 26, 1970—some 3 years and 7 months since his last professional bout.

The following year, the Supreme Court of the United States finally overturned his conviction. The court held that Ali's refusal of the draft was valid due to his sincere religious beliefs. The king of the ring was back.

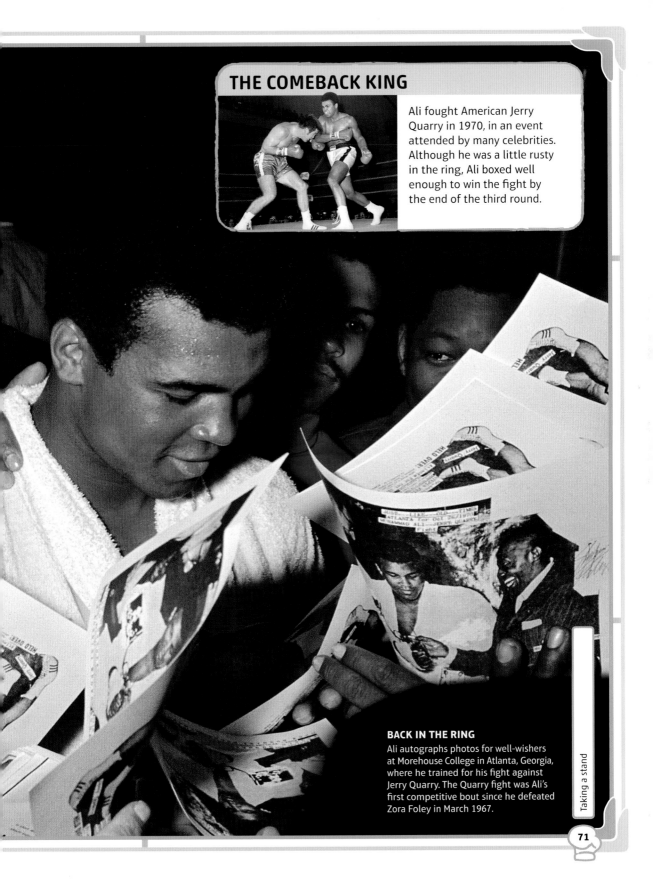

THE COMEBACK KING

Ali fought American Jerry Quarry in 1970, in an event attended by many celebrities. Although he was a little rusty in the ring, Ali boxed well enough to win the fight by the end of the third round.

BACK IN THE RING

Ali autographs photos for well-wishers at Morehouse College in Atlanta, Georgia, where he trained for his fight against Jerry Quarry. The Quarry fight was Ali's first competitive bout since he defeated Zora Foley in March 1967.

Taking a stand

THE KING RETURNS

After his exile, Muhammad Ali returned to boxing in 1970. In this phase of his career, he endured his first professional defeats, and enjoyed some of his most memorable triumphs. He became the world champion for a second, and then a third time.

RECLAIMING HIS THRONE
Ali raises his arms to salute the crowd in Kinshasa, Zaire (now the Democratic Republic of the Congo), before his 1974 World Championship fight against George Foreman. This bout would go down in history for Ali's unusual tactics and how he won.

FIGHT OF THE CENTURY

Muhammad Ali's first fight with Joe Frazier was also his first title bout since his exile, and it captured the imagination of boxing fans worldwide. The venue of the fight, Madison Square Garden, was packed. The fight even attracted the famous entertainer Frank Sinatra, who gained entry as a press photographer for *Life* magazine.

Ali was unbeaten in 31 fights, Frazier in 26—no one knew who would prevail. It was a close call through much of this epic contest. Ali dominated the first three rounds, before Frazier roared back with some punishing punches, one of which, in the 11th round, rocked Ali and caused his jaw to swell up alarmingly.

Still not at his peak level of fitness, Ali was tired and slowing dramatically. He suffered his first knockdown since 1963 in the 15th round of the fight, as Frazier's left hook crashed onto Ali's chin. Somehow, Ali managed to get to his feet and finish the fight, but few disagreed with the judges awarding the victory to Frazier.

> ❝ HE **AIN'T THE GREATEST**. HE'S BEEN **KIDDIN' HIMSELF** AND THE WORLD. ❞
>
> – Joe Frazier after his victory

The king returns

FIGHT FILE

OPPONENT: Joe Frazier, age 27, American

DATE AND PLACE: March 8, 1971, Madison Square Garden, New York City, New York

RESULT: Ali lost by unanimous decision (15th round)

The fight was broadcast in **12 languages** to around **300 million TV viewers**.

JOE FRAZIER

One of 13 children from a poor South Carolina family, Joe Frazier built a glittering amateur boxing career, which included three national Golden Gloves titles and a 1964 Olympic gold medal.

On turning professional in 1965, Frazier won his first 11 fights, all by knockouts. In 1970, he defeated Jimmy Ellis to become world champion. His reign included a memorable defeat of Muhammad Ali (see pages 74–75), and lasted until 1973 when he was defeated by George Foreman, who knocked Frazier down six times in under two rounds.

After two further epic bouts with Ali, Frazier suffered a second loss to Foreman in 1976 and retired from boxing. He returned briefly in 1981, drawing a fight with Floyd "Jumbo" Cummings, before retiring for good. Frazier trained his daughter, Jacqui, who won her first world title in 2001, making them the first father-daughter pair of boxing world champions. Frazier died on November 7, 2011, in Pennsylvania.

FORMIDABLE FORCE
Frazier works a punch ball hard before his 1970 world title defense against American boxer Bob Foster. Stocky and powerfully built, Frazier boxed in a crouched posture. From this position, he would constantly press forward, pressurizing his opponents and launching his crunching hook shots.

DEER LAKE CAMP

Seeking time away from the limelight to train and focus properly, in 1972 Muhammad Ali constructed his purpose-built Deer Lake training camp in the Pennsylvania countryside. Here, he prepared for most of his remaining fights.

Ali first came across the Deer Lake area when training in a basic gym there owned by Bernie Pollack, the manager of Ali's 1967 opponent, Ernie Terrell.

Deer Lake contained more than a dozen wooden buildings. These included a dining hall, a mosque, a barn for horses that Ali sometimes rode, and a gym where he worked on his own or with sparring partners.

Despite its relative seclusion, Deer Lake saw many celebrity visitors, such as the actor Sylvester Stallone, the artist Andy Warhol, and singers Elvis Presley and Frank Sinatra.

In 1997, the **camp was sold** and turned into a **bed and breakfast** called the Butterfly & Bee.

HARD AT WORK

Ali chops a tree at the camp as part of his training regime, which included early morning runs through the hills, sometimes accompanied by local children. Ali also had boulders dotted around the camp painted with names of famous and legendary boxers he admired, for motivation and inspiration.

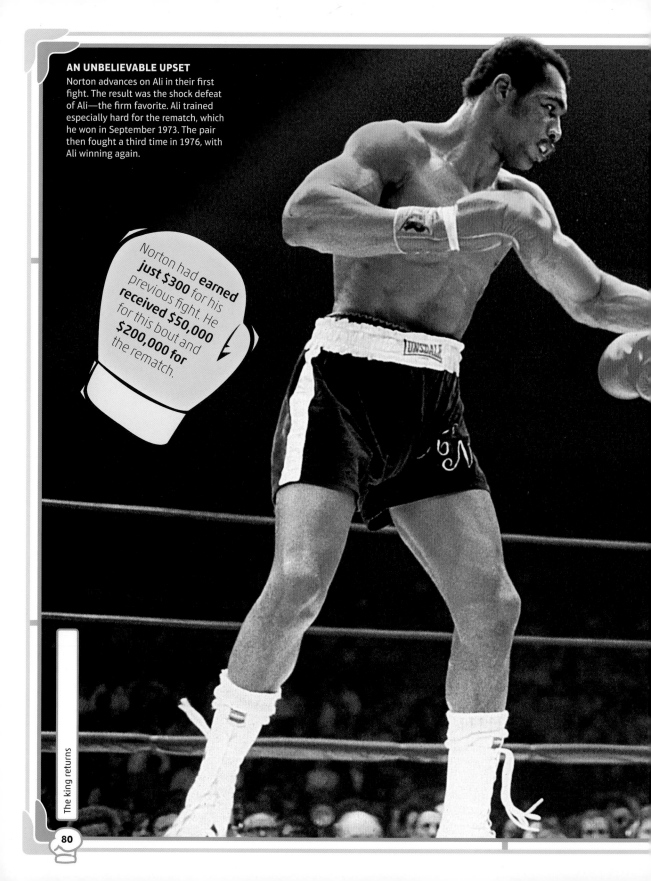

AN UNBELIEVABLE UPSET
Norton advances on Ali in their first fight. The result was the shock defeat of Ali—the firm favorite. Ali trained especially hard for the rematch, which he won in September 1973. The pair then fought a third time in 1976, with Ali winning again.

Norton had **earned just $300** for his previous fight. He **received $50,000** for this bout and **$200,000 for** the rematch.

JAW BREAKER

Muhammad Ali's first fight against Ken Norton was his 11th bout since his 1971 loss to Joe Frazier. These fights included rematches against Floyd Patterson and Jerry Quarry, as well as one against old Louisville rival, Jimmy Ellis—all of which he had won.

However, Ali underestimated his next opponent—Norton—calling him "an amateur." Ali even played golf when he should have been training in the week before the fight. Norton was an ex-US Marine who possessed a powerful physique, but few thought he would last long against Ali.

They were wrong. Norton proved a dangerous opponent, who crossed his arms in defense and threw his jab upward from waist height—most boxers jab with their arm at shoulder level. This made him tricky to fight against.

Norton also had a sledgehammer of a punch, breaking Ali's jaw during the fight. Ali bravely boxed on for the rest of the 12-round bout, but he lost the fight in a close contest.

FIGHT FILE

OPPONENT: Ken Norton, age 29, American

DATE AND PLACE: March 31, 1973, Sports Arena, San Diego, California

RESULT: Ali lost by split decision (12th round)

DON KING

Controversial and garrulous, boxing promoter Don King grew up in Cleveland, Ohio. From a young age, he became involved in running illegal betting games. In 1967, he was imprisoned, but was released in 1971.

Entering the business of boxing in 1971, he convinced Muhammad Ali to box in a charity match to raise funds for a Cleveland hospital in 1972. Two years later, King arranged one of Ali's biggest fights—the "Rumble in the Jungle" against George Foreman. He guaranteed each boxer a record-breaking $5 million, despite not having the funds himself. So, he had to turn to the president of Zaire (now Democratic Republic of the Congo), Mobutu Sese Seko (see page 86), to sponsor the fight.

King would go on to promote seven of Ali's bouts and more than 500 world championship fights in the 1980s and 1990s. These fights featured boxers such as Mike Tyson, Roy Jones Jr., and Larry Holmes.

> **DON** IS THE **ONLY PERSON**…
> WHO CAN PROMOTE
> A FIGHT BY **FORCE OF
> PERSONALITY**. "
>
> *– Lou DiBella, boxing promoter*

In 1994, Don King **promoted** a record **47 world championship fights** in a single year.

PRE-FIGHT BRAWL

Tensions were rising between Muhammad Ali and Joe Frazier before their scheduled match in 1974.

Ali's previous contest against the Dutchman Rudi Lubbers had been so easy that he even spoke to ringside reporters in between rounds. However, Frazier was a far tougher opponent.

Ali stepped up the war of words before the contest, accusing Frazier of not caring about issues faced by African-Americans. Frazier became increasingly angry and bitter at the verbal abuse he suffered.

The animosity between the pair spilled over during a TV show hosted by Howard Cosell (see pages 62–63) two days before their fight. Ali and Frazier got into a brawl and rolled around on the studio floor.

Both of the boxers were fined $5,000 for the ugly scene, which only heightened interest in their forthcoming clash.

"FIGHT" BEFORE THE FIGHT
Ali taunts Frazier (far left) at a press meet in New York City to announce their fight. Ali did this despite Frazier having spoken to politicians in the late 1960s, urging them to help Ali regain his boxing licence.

SUPER FIGHT II

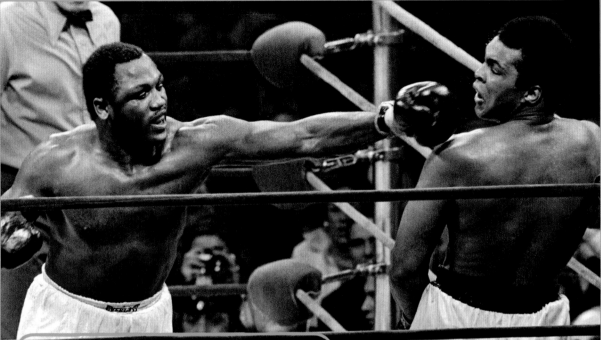

Promoted as "Super Fight II," the second fight between Muhammad Ali and Joe Frazier took place in January 1974. The winner of this 12-round bout would face the world champion, George Foreman, in a heavyweight title fight.

With so much at stake, both fighters were eager to prove themselves. In the ring, the fight ebbed and flowed with both boxers having spells when they appeared on top.

Ali looked sharp and effective in the early rounds, and then used all his cunning and ring craft to hold Frazier at bay in the later rounds. Ali won, avenging his 1971 defeat (see pages 74–75).

FIGHT FILE

 OPPONENT: Joe Frazier, age 30, American

 DATE AND PLACE: January 28, 1974, Madison Square Garden, New York City, New York

 RESULT: Ali won by unanimous decision (12th round)

A CROWD FAVORITE

Ali stokes up a large number of Zairians by pretending that he can't hear them. Before his fight with George Foreman on October 30, 1974, Ali drew large crowds wherever he went.

Ali's former trainer and opponent, **Archie Moore**, was **one of Foreman's trainers** for the fight.

MOBUTU SESE SEKO

George Foreman (right), wearing traditional African clothes, meets Zaire's former president Mobutu Sese Seko. A former soldier who seized power in a 1965 military coup, Mobutu remained as dictator until 1997. Mobutu used his country's money to sponsor the fight.

GETTING READY TO RUMBLE

In the summer of 1974, Muhammad Ali and George Foreman, the reigning world heavyweight champion, flew to Zaire (now the Democratic Republic of the Congo) to train for the richest fight in boxing history at the time—known as the "Rumble in the Jungle." Each boxer would receive $5 million for the bout.

The fight was scheduled for September 24, but was delayed after Foreman was injured in training. This left the champion to recuperate and brood, while Ali—the challenger—enjoyed whipping up support among the local people and firing out comments and speeches to reporters.

Ali's camp, though, was tense. Foreman boasted a 40–0 fight record, which included wins against the only two boxers to defeat Ali—Ken Norton and Joe Frazier. Both of them had lasted for just two rounds against Foreman.

Not since the first fight against Sonny Liston (see pages 48–49) had Ali's friends and training team feared as much for their boxer's safety.

The king returns

RUMBLE IN THE JUNGLE

At 4 am in Kinshasa, Zaire (now the Democratic Republic of the Congo), 60,000 roaring spectators were getting ready to watch Muhammad Ali fight George Foreman. By some reports, another one billion people around the world tuned in to their television sets to watch the fight known as the "Rumble in the Jungle."

Ali's fans chanted ringside in the local language of Langala, "Ali, bomaye!" (Ali, kill him!), but the 32-year-old Ali was the underdog against the reigning world heavyweight champion, 25-year-old Foreman. In fact, many boxing experts feared for Ali's safety against the formidable Foreman, who came into the bout unbeaten in 40 consecutive fights.

Foreman started confidently, landing hard punches on Ali, who relied on his quick jabs and lightning footwork. In the second round, Ali did something completely different, shocking even. While his trainer Angelo Dundee (see pages 30–31) watched in disbelief from his corner, Ali let Foreman hit him again and again, as he slumped against the ropes. Ali continued with this strategy, nicknamed "rope-a-dope," until round eight. His body hurt, of course, but Foreman became exhausted. Then, with a flurry of punches ending in a right hook, Ali sent Foreman to the canvas. Against all odds, Ali was the world heavyweight champion for the second time.

After the match, Ali **admitted** that he had **never been hit so hard** in his life.

MOMENTS FROM VICTORY
Ali stands back as the referee, Zack Clayton, calls the count over Foreman, who finds himself lying on the canvas. The crowd is on its feet, as they loudly cheer for Ali's return as champion.

FIGHT FILE

OPPONENT: George Foreman, age 25, American

DATE AND PLACE: October 30, 1974, 20th of May Stadium, Kinshasa, Zaire (Democratic Republic of the Congo)

RESULT: Ali won by knockout (8th round)

The king returns

> **AT HIS PEAK** FOREMAN HAD A TRUE **AURA OF INVINCIBILITY**. JUST WATCHING GEORGE TRAIN… WAS A TERRIFYING EXPERIENCE. THE **RAFTERS SHOOK, THE FLOOR RUMBLED**. 🙶
>
> – Monte D. Cox, boxing historian

Foreman **named his five sons George**, so they would **"have something in common!"**

INSPIRING TEENAGERS
Foreman poses with his world heavyweight championship belt at a high school in California in 1973. He was on a tour to meet and speak to school children.

GEORGE FOREMAN

In 1973, the formidable George Foreman won his first world heavyweight championship belt in sensational fashion, defeating Joe Frazier by knocking him down six times in under two rounds.

Foreman defended his title in similarly brutal fashion, knocking Ken Norton out in two rounds. Then, in 1974, he faced Muhammad Ali in the "Rumble in the Jungle" (see pages 88–89), which resulted in a shocking loss.

Foreman first retired from boxing in 1977 and became a Christian minister, before making an unexpected comeback to the ring in 1987. Seven years later, at the age of 45, he became the oldest world heavyweight champion, when he beat Michael Moorer in 1994.

In the mid-1990s, the boxer had also lent his name to and promoted the George Foreman Grill for cooking burgers, with sales exceeding 100 million units worldwide.

Foreman won 76 of his 81 fights between 1969–1999, with 68 victories by knockout. He was knocked out only once—by Ali, whom he became close to in later years.

THRILLA IN MANILA

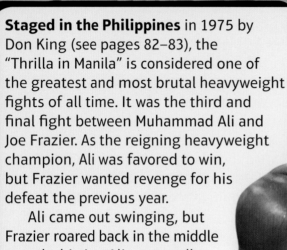

Staged in the Philippines in 1975 by Don King (see pages 82–83), the "Thrilla in Manila" is considered one of the greatest and most brutal heavyweight fights of all time. It was the third and final fight between Muhammad Ali and Joe Frazier. As the reigning heavyweight champion, Ali was favored to win, but Frazier wanted revenge for his defeat the previous year.

Ali came out swinging, but Frazier roared back in the middle rounds, hitting Ali repeatedly with his trademark left hook. Ali appeared exhausted in the ninth and tenth rounds, but then exploded into life, landing flurries of vicious punches.

By the 14th round, Frazier's right eye had completely closed and his trainer, Eddie Futch, ended the fight to stop further punishment. Ali, who had been close to quitting himself, raised his arms wearily in triumph before collapsing on the canvas.

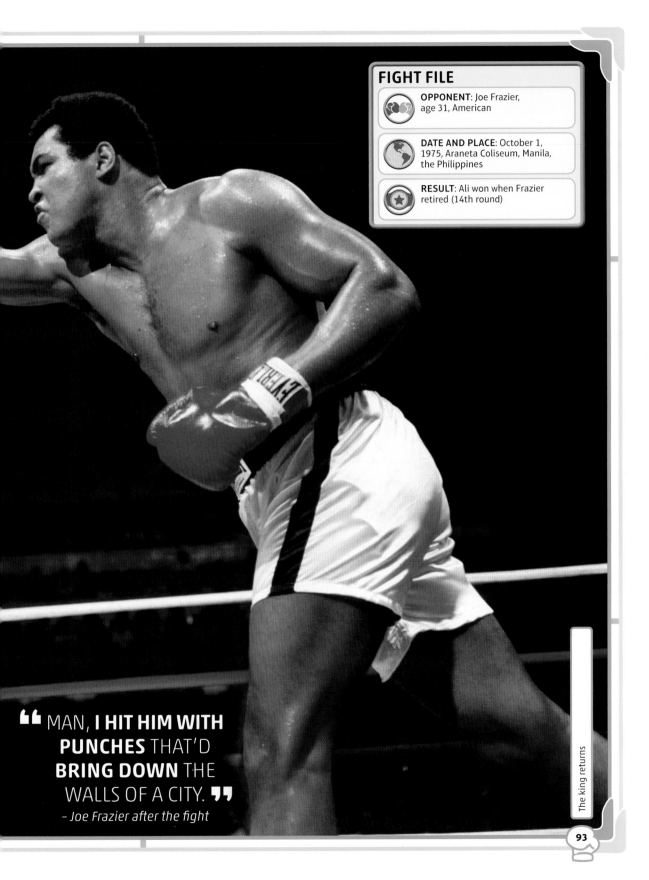

OPPONENT: Joe Frazier, age 31, American

DATE AND PLACE: October 1, 1975, Araneta Coliseum, Manila, the Philippines

RESULT: Ali won when Frazier retired (14th round)

" MAN, **I HIT HIM WITH PUNCHES** THAT'D **BRING DOWN** THE WALLS OF A CITY. "
– Joe Frazier after the fight

The king returns

ALI, THE ACTOR

Muhammad Ali's first appearance on film was a small role in the 1962 movie *Requiem for a Heavyweight*, which starred actors Anthony Quinn and Mickey Rooney.

Ali's 1975 autobiography, *The Greatest: My Own Story*, written with Richard Durham, was turned into a movie called *The Greatest* two years later. Ali starred in this movie as himself, as did his brother, Rahaman, and his cornerman Drew Bundini Brown (see page 42).

In 1979, Ali took on the lead role in *Freedom Road*, a movie aired over two nights on television. Ali played the fictional Gideon Jackson, a former slave who eventually became a United States senator after fighting as a soldier in the Civil War.

ON SET
Ali waits on the set of *Freedom Road* in 1978, in costume and with a grey beard. He acted alongside Kris Kristoffersen and received mixed reviews for his performance in the four-hour long movie.

THE MISMATCH

In 1976, Muhammad Ali and Japanese wrestler and mixed martial artist Antonio Inoki took part in a strange exhibition match. The mixed martial arts (MMA) experiment took place at the Budokan Arena in Tokyo, Japan, and Ali received $6 million to fight.

The contest failed in its attempts to mix Ali's and Inoki's very different styles. Inoki spent much of the 15-round bout on his back, throwing kicks at Ali, who in return was only able to land a handful of punches. The event ended in a draw amid a chorus of boos from the crowd.

Afterward, Ali suffered with blood clots in his legs that affected his movement. However, the two combatants remained friends and Ali flew to Japan in 1998 to witness Inoki's last bout before he retired.

❝ ALI WAS A SHOWMAN, BUT THIS **WASN'T MUCH OF A SHOW**, AND IT PUT HIS ENTIRE **CAREER IN JEOPARDY.** **❞**

– *Ferdie Pacheco, Ali's doctor*

The king returns

REGAINING THE BELT

Muhammad Ali fought Leon Spinks for the second time in September 1978. Their first bout, in February of that year, had seen a shocking defeat for Ali at the hands of the 1976 Olympic gold medallist in only his eighth professional fight.

This defeat stung Ali. He even went on a training run early in the morning after the fight, beginning his punishing preparations for a rematch straight away.

For the second fight, a crowd of 63,350 people packed the Louisiana Superdome, and most of them were relieved when they saw a noticeably sharper Ali in action. Ali lost the fifth round when penalized for holding on to his opponent, but was rarely in trouble.

Spinks found it hard to land many strong blows as Ali rolled back the years with flashes of fleet footwork and short flurries of stinging punches. To choruses of "Ali, Ali" from fans, the judges awarded him the fight, making Ali—at the age of 36—the first boxer in history to win the world heavyweight championship three times.

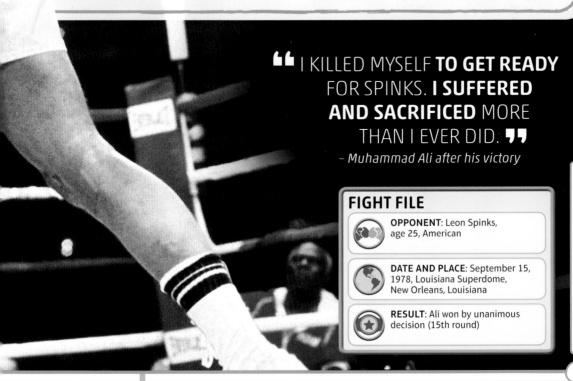

❝ I KILLED MYSELF TO GET READY FOR SPINKS. I SUFFERED AND SACRIFICED MORE THAN I EVER DID. ❞
– Muhammad Ali after his victory

FIGHT FILE

OPPONENT: Leon Spinks, age 25, American

DATE AND PLACE: September 15, 1978, Louisiana Superdome, New Orleans, Louisiana

RESULT: Ali won by unanimous decision (15th round)

The king returns

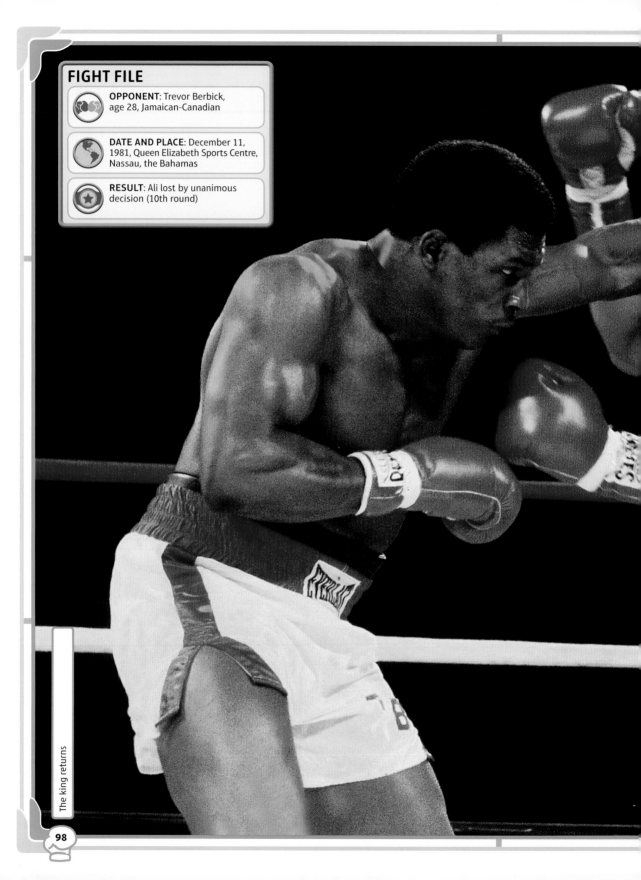

FIGHT FILE

OPPONENT: Trevor Berbick, age 28, Jamaican-Canadian

DATE AND PLACE: December 11, 1981, Queen Elizabeth Sports Centre, Nassau, the Bahamas

RESULT: Ali lost by unanimous decision (10th round)

THE FINAL FIGHT

Muhammad Ali retired from boxing for the first time in 1979. However, he returned to the ring a year later to fight Larry Holmes. Ali suffered a crushing defeat in this one-sided contest, which was stopped after the 10th round by his trainer, Angelo Dundee (see pages 30–31).

After this loss, many in Ali's entourage asked him to retire for good. They worried about Ali's well-being, and the damage done to him by two decades of taking blows from many of the world's hardest-punching boxers. Yet Ali persisted and traveled to the Bahamas to fight Trevor Berbick, a contest marred by concerns for his health, and dogged by poor organization—the promoters forgot to supply a stopwatch or bell to signal the end of each round!

While Ali won the fifth and sixth rounds, he faded as the fight progressed and had to use all his willpower to avoid a knockout against an overpowering Berbick. No one doubted the judges' decision at the end of ten rounds. This was Ali's fifth defeat in his glittering 61 fight career. It was now time to hang up the gloves.

> **"** I THINK I'M **TOO OLD**.
> **I WAS SLOW**. I WAS WEAK. **"**
> – Muhammad Ali after the fight

LIFE AFTER BOXING

Muhammad Ali's life after retirement from boxing was overshadowed by Parkinson's disease, but this did not prevent him from supporting charitable causes. He traveled around the world to promote peace and cooperation between people.

A WELCOME EMBRACE
American oil drilling consultant Royce Smart embraces Ali on December 4, 1990, at New York's John F. Kennedy Airport. The former boxing champion had helped secure Smart's release from Iraq.

ALI, THE AMBASSADOR

From the late 1970s Muhammad Ali had become a celebrity, in and out of the ring, and he criss-crossed the globe to support the charities and causes he believed in.

At the request of the former American president Jimmy Carter, Ali traveled to many African nations to encourage them to join the United States and other countries in not sending athletes to the 1980 Olympics, held in the Soviet Union (now Russia). The boycott was a protest at the Soviet Union's invasion of Afghanistan in 1979.

After retiring from boxing in 1981, Ali continued his work as a non-official ambassador. For example, he visited Iraq in 1990, and met with many senior Iraqi politicians, including the country's president at the time, Saddam Hussein. Though Ali's three-day trip was heavily criticized by the media, and met with disapproval by the United States government, it resulted in the release of 15 American workers who were being held as hostages in Iraq.

Ali's many humanitarian visits included trips to meet famine victims in Bangladesh and travels to Africa to promote peace and health initiatives. He also visited China three times to help revive boxing in that country.

> **❝** I'M NOT GOING TO LET **MUHAMMAD ALI RETURN** TO THE U.S. WITHOUT HAVING A NUMBER OF THE **AMERICAN CITIZENS ACCOMPANYING HIM. ❞**
> – Former Iraqi president Saddam Hussein after meeting with Ali

" I HAVE WATCHED HIM **FACE THE DISEASE WITH GRACE** AND HUMOR... **INSPIRED COUNTLESS PATIENTS** TO DO THE SAME. **"**

– Dr. Holly Shill, director of the Muhammad Ali Parkinson's Center at the Barrow Neurological Institute

FIGHTING TO HELP
Ali and actor Michael J. Fox (right) joke around before a 2002 United States Congress committee investigating Parkinson's disease. Fox was also diagnosed with Parkinson's in 1991, seven years after Ali had learned he had the disease.

FIGHT WITH PARKINSON'S

As early as the late 1970s, some people close to Muhammad Ali had been alarmed by the boxer's slowed movement and slurred speech. Both of these are classic symptoms of Parkinson's disease.

This disease destroys cells in a small area of the brain that plays a major role in movement and muscle control. People with Parkinson's experience a loss of stability and balance, uncontrollable shaking, difficulty in sleeping and swallowing, and changes in their speech, among other symptoms.

Despite suffering from the effects of the disease, Ali worked hard to increase awareness of Parkinson's. In 1997, he also raised funds to help open and run a center within the Barrow Neurological Institute, in Phoenix, Arizona, to research this disease.

There is still no cure for Parkinson's, which affects more than 10 million people worldwide. However, medicines and surgeries can help control and relieve some of the symptoms.

❝ **EVERYONE** WHO MEETS LONNIE **LOVES HER**, BECAUSE **SHE'S NICE**, SHE'S SMART, **AND SHE LOVES ALI.** ❞
– Howard Bingham

LONNIE ALI

Muhammad Ali and Yolanda "Lonnie" Williams became a couple in the 1980s. In fact, Lonnie had grown up on the same Louisville street as Ali's parents in the 1960s, and their mothers were good friends.

Lonnie studied psychology at Vanderbilt University, Tennessee, and moved to Los Angeles in 1982 to pursue a masters in business administration at the University of California. She also became Ali's caregiver, as he was suffering from Parkinson's disease (see pages 104–105). The pair married in 1986, and adopted a five-month-old boy, Asaad, in the same year.

Lonnie accompanied her husband on his many trips, and helped to protect and promote his business interests as well as the charities and causes they both supported.

On their 19th wedding anniversary, in November 2005, the couple opened a museum and cultural venue called the Muhammad Ali Center in Louisville.

MEETING MANDELA

The South African statesman Nelson Mandela first met Muhammad Ali in 1990, the same year that Mandela was released after serving 27 years in a South African prison for supporting the anti-apartheid movement.

As a young man, Mandela had trained as a boxer. However, he was more interested in the science of the sport and the dedication it required than the actual fights.

While in prison, Mandela followed Ali's career. He was impressed not only with Ali's boxing mastery, but also with how he used his personality and fame to challenge the injustices he faced in life.

The pair met a few more times, including in South Africa in 1993, a year before Mandela was elected the country's first black president. Mandela died in Johannesburg on December 5, 2013, at the age of 95.

COMMON CAUSES
Mandela throws a mock punch at Ali during their meeting in Dublin, Republic of Ireland, to promote the 2003 Special Olympics. The pair collaborated on a number of initiatives, including treatment for and prevention of HIV/AIDS.

Life after boxing

LIGHTING THE OLYMPIC FLAME

The climax of the Opening Ceremony at the 1996 Summer Olympic Games in Atlanta, Georgia, involved a flaming torch being passed between former Olympic heroes, but the identity of the final athlete had been kept a closely-guarded secret.

It was revealed when American champion swimmer, Janet Evans, passed the torch to Muhammad Ali, and the entire stadium and millions of television viewers worldwide gasped. Parkinson's disease (see pages 104–105) had clearly taken a toll on Ali, who fought hard to control his shaking body. He successfully lit the Olympic flame—it was a powerful and emotional moment.

During the Atlanta Games, Ali also received a replacement for his 1960 Olympic gold medal (see pages 22–23), which he had lost.

> **❝ I WAS WEEPING LIKE A BABY** SEEING HIS HANDS SHAKE. NO MATTER WHAT IT TOOK, **THE FLAME WOULD BE LIT. ❞**
> – Former US president Bill Clinton on watching Ali light the flame

Life after boxing

LAILA ALI

In 2001, Laila fought **Jacqui Frazier-Lyde**—the **daughter of Ali's rival** Joe Frazier— and **won**.

Muhammad Ali's sixth child, Laila Ali, completed a degree in business and owned a nail salon before entering the world of boxing. She was inspired to do so after watching an entertaining women's boxing match in 1996 between American boxer Christy Martin and Deidre Gogarty from Ireland.

At first, Ali opposed the idea, fearing for his daughter's safety. But Laila shared the same independent streak as her father, who eventually relented and attended many of his daughter's fights. In Laila's first bout in 1999, it took her just 31 seconds to overcome American April Fowler.

When Laila ended her career in 2007, she retired with an unbeaten 24-fight record. Along the way, she won five different world title belts— one at light-heavyweight and four in the super-middleweight division.

PRESIDENTIAL MEDAL OF FREEDOM

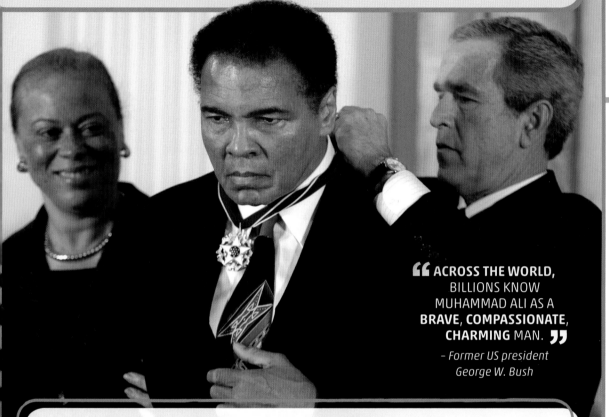

66 ACROSS THE WORLD, BILLIONS KNOW MUHAMMAD ALI AS A **BRAVE, COMPASSIONATE, CHARMING** MAN. **99**

– Former US president George W. Bush

In November 2005, Muhammad Ali received the highest civilian award in the United States—the Presidential Medal of Freedom. Former recipients of this award include astronaut Neil Armstrong, scientist Stephen Hawking, and civil rights activist Rosa Parks.

Ali had traveled with his wife, Lonnie, to the White House in Washington, D.C., where the then president George W. Bush greeted him and placed the medal around his neck. In his speech, Bush praised the boxer and stated, "The American people are proud to call Muhammad Ali one of our own."

Ali was further honored the following month in Germany. He flew to Berlin to receive the Otto Hahn Peace Medal for his work with the United Nations and on civil rights.

A LIGHT GOES OUT

After battling breathing difficulties and failing health, Muhammad Ali died at the Osborn Medical Center in Scottsdale, Arizona, on June 3, 2016. He was 74 years old.

Ali's death dominated global news and tributes poured in from all over the world. A week after his death, a motorcade carrying his coffin drove through his childhood hometown of Louisville. Thousands of people lined the route, which followed the road taken by 18-year-old Cassius Clay when he had returned home in triumph with his 1960 Olympic gold medal (see pages 22–23).

After a private burial, a public memorial service was attended by about 15,000 people, including former US president Bill Clinton, and many boxing legends such as Larry Holmes and George Foreman (see pages 90–91).

" MUHAMMAD ALI **SHOOK UP THE WORLD**. AND THE **WORLD IS BETTER FOR IT**. **"**
— *Former US president Barack Obama*

REMEMBERING ALI

200 → 270

West 33rd St

MADISON SQUARE GARDEN

Muhammad Ali
Way

"THE GREATEST"
1942-2016

ONE WAY
DEPT OF TRANSPORTATION

1:53

DISON SQUARE

Muhammad Ali was many things— a loyal friend, a doting father, a man of faith, and a sporting legend. He also had a sparkling, sharp-witted personality.

As a skilled and charismatic fighter, Ali redefined how boxing was viewed by many and attracted legions of new fans to the sport. Though his stance on the Vietnam War (see pages 58–59) cost him three-and-a-half years of his career, he stood by his beliefs and emerged as a force for change.

Ali is admired the world over for his unflinching principles as well as for the bravery and dignity he showed while battling Parkinson's disease toward the end of his life.

6

REFERENCE

Muhammad Ali's professional boxing career spanned more than two decades, with him winning 56 of his 61 fights. The following pages give Ali's entire fight record and highlight some less well-known facts about his life and examples of his sharp, sometimes profound, wit.

A HERO FOR ALL AGES
Ali signs autographs at a children's
play group in London, UK, in 1966.
He visited them just six days
before his second fight against
British boxer Henry Cooper.

ALI'S LIFE

Muhammad Ali led a fascinating and, at times, controversial life during a period of great change in the United States and the world. Here is a timeline of key moments and events in the life of "The Greatest."

MARCH 6, 1964
Cassius Clay officially changes his name to Muhammad Ali shortly after winning his first heavyweight championship belt.

MARCH 22, 1967
Ali fights and defeats Zora Folley. This is Ali's last fight before being stripped of his title and boxing license as he refused to be drafted into the US Army for the Vietnam War.

JUNE 28, 1971
In the court case of *Cassius Marcellus Clay Jr. vs. United States*, the Supreme Court reverses Ali's 1967 conviction for refusing the draft.

1954
A 12-year-old Clay joins the Columbia Gym in Louisville, run by police officer Joe Martin.

1959
Clay wins his first Intercity Golden Gloves amateur title.

1940 ──────────────────── 1960

JANUARY 17, 1942
Cassius Marcellus Clay Jr. is born in Louisville, Kentucky.

SEPTEMBER 5, 1960
At the age of 18, Clay wins the gold medal in the light heavyweight boxing division at the Rome Olympics. He participates in his first professional fight later that year.

OCTOBER 1, 1975
Ali fights Joe Frazier for a third and final time in the Philippines and wins, in a fight known as the "Thrilla in Manila."

OCTOBER 3, 1980

Ali comes out of retirement to face Larry Holmes at Caesars Palace in Las Vegas, Nevada. Holmes overwhelms Ali and the fight is stopped after 10 rounds.

NOVEMBER 19, 2005

The Muhammad Ali Center—a non-profit museum and cultural center—is opened by Muhammad and Lonnie Ali in Louisville, Kentucky.

1984

Ali is officially diagnosed with Parkinson's disease after five days of tests at a New York medical center.

1990

Ali travels to Iraq and helps secure the release of 15 Americans held hostage by the Iraqi regime led by Saddam Hussein.

JULY 27, 2012

Ali attends the Olympic Games held in London, UK, as an honorary guest.

1980   2000   2020

NOVEMBER 19, 1986

Ali marries his fourth wife, Yolanda "Lonnie" Williams.

JUNE 3, 2016

Ali dies at the age of 74 in Phoenix, Arizona, after a brief period of illness.

JULY 19, 1996

Ali lights the Olympic flame at the Opening Ceremony for the 1996 Olympics in Atlanta, Georgia. The event is viewed by almost 40 million people in the US, and millions more worldwide.

2001

The Hollywood motion picture, *Ali*, is released, starring American actor Will Smith in the title role.

ALI'S FIGHT FILE

Fight 1: October 29, 1960
Opponent: Tunney Hunsaker (USA)
Venue: Freedom Hall, Louisville, Kentucky
Result: Clay won by unanimous decision (6th round)

Fight 2: December 27, 1960
Opponent: Herbert Siler (USA)
Venue: Auditorium, Miami Beach, Florida
Result: Clay won by technical knockout (4th round)

Fight 3: January 17, 1961
Opponent: Anthony Esperti (USA)
Venue: Auditorium, Miami Beach, Florida
Result: Clay won by technical knockout (3rd round)

Fight 4: February 7, 1961
Opponent: Jimmy Robinson (USA)
Venue: Convention Center, Miami Beach, Florida
Result: Clay won by technical knockout (1st round)

Fight 5: February 21, 1961
Opponent: Donnie Fleeman (USA)
Venue: Auditorium, Miami Beach, Florida
Result: Clay won when Fleeman retired (6th round)

Fight 6: April 19, 1961
Opponent: LaMar Clark (USA)
Venue: Freedom Hall, Louisville, Kentucky
Result: Clay won by knockout (2nd round)

Fight 7: June 26, 1961
Opponent: Duke Sabedong (USA)
Venue: Convention Center, Las Vegas, Nevada
Result: Clay won by unanimous decision (10th round)

Fight 8: July 22, 1961
Opponent: Alonzo Johnson (USA)
Venue: Freedom Hall, Louisville, Kentucky
Result: Clay won by unanimous decision (10th round)

Fight 9: October 7, 1961
Opponent: Alex Miteff (Argentina)
Venue: Freedom Hall, Louisville, Kentucky
Result: Clay won by technical knockout (6th round)

Fight 10: November 29, 1961
Opponent: Willi Besmanoff (Germany)
Venue: Freedom Hall, Louisville, Kentucky
Result: Clay won by technical knockout (7th round)

Fight 11: February 10, 1962
Opponent: Sonny Banks (USA)
Venue: Madison Square Garden, New York City, New York
Result: Clay won by technical knockout (4th round)

Fight 12: February 28, 1962
Opponent: Don Warner (USA)
Venue: Convention Center, Miami Beach, Florida
Result: Clay won by technical knockout (4th round)

Fight 13: April 23, 1962
Opponent: George Logan (USA)
Venue: Sports Arena, Los Angeles, California
Result: Clay won by technical knockout (4th round)

Fight 14: May 19, 1962
Opponent: Billy Daniels (USA)
Venue: St. Nicholas Arena, New York City, New York
Result: Clay won by technical knockout (7th round)

Fight 15: July 20, 1962
Opponent: Alejandro Lavorante (Argentina)
Venue: Sports Arena, Los Angeles, California
Result: Clay won by knockout (5th round)

Fight 16: November 15, 1962
Opponent: Archie Moore (USA)
Venue: Sports Arena, Los Angeles, California
Result: Clay won by technical knockout (4th round)

Fight 17: January 24, 1963
Opponent: Charles Powell (USA)
Venue: Civic Arena, Pittsburgh, Pennsylvania
Result: Clay won by knockout (3rd round)

Fight 18: March 13, 1963
Opponent: Doug Jones (USA)
Venue: Madison Square Garden, New York City, New York
Result: Clay won by unanimous decision (10th round)

Fight 19: June 18, 1963
Opponent: Henry Cooper (UK)
Venue: Wembley Stadium, London, UK
Result: Clay won by technical knockout (5th round)

Fight 20: February 25, 1964
Opponent: Sonny Liston (USA)
Venue: Convention Center, Miami Beach, Florida
Result: Clay won when Liston retired (6th round)

Fight 21: May 25, 1965
Opponent: Sonny Liston (USA)
Venue: Central Maine Civic Center, Lewiston, Maine
Result: Ali won by knockout (1st round)

Fight 22: November 22, 1965
Opponent: Floyd Patterson (USA)
Venue: Convention Center, Las Vegas, Nevada
Result: Ali won by technical knockout (12th round)

Fight 23: March 29, 1966
Opponent: George Chuvalo (Canada)
Venue: Maple Leaf Gardens, Toronto, Canada
Result: Ali won by unanimous decision (15th round)

Fight 24: May 21, 1966
Opponent: Henry Cooper (UK)
Venue: Arsenal Football Stadium, London, UK
Result: Ali won by technical knockout (6th round)

Fight 25: August 6, 1966
Opponent: Brian London (UK)
Venue: Earls Court Arena, London, UK
Result: Ali won by knockout (3rd round)

Fight 26: September 10, 1966
Opponent: Karl Mildenberger (Germany)
Venue: Waldstadion/Radrennbahn, Frankfurt, Germany
Result: Ali won by technical knockout (12th round)

Fight 27: November 14, 1966
Opponent: Cleveland Williams (USA)
Venue: Astrodome, Houston, Texas
Result: Ali won by technical knockout (3rd round)

Fight 28: February 6, 1967
Opponent: Ernie Terrell (USA)
Venue: Astrodome, Houston, Texas
Result: Ali won by unanimous decision (15th round)

Fight 29: March 22, 1967
Opponent: Zora Folley (USA)
Venue: Madison Square Garden, New York City, New York
Result: Ali won by knockout (7th round)

Fight 30: October 26, 1970
Opponent: Jerry Quarry (USA)
Venue: City Auditorium, Atlanta, Georgia
Result: Ali won when Quarry retired (3rd round)

Fight 31: December 7, 1970
Opponent: Oscar Bonavena (Argentina)
Venue: Madison Square Garden, New York City, New York
Result: Ali won by technical knockout (15th round)

Fight 32: March 8, 1971
Opponent: Joe Frazier (USA)
Venue: Madison Square Garden, New York City, New York
Result: Ali lost by unanimous decision (15th round)

Fight 33: July 26, 1971
Opponent: Jimmy Ellis (USA)
Venue: Astrodome, Houston, Texas
Result: Ali won by technical knockout (12th round)

Fight 34: November 17, 1971
Opponent: Buster Mathis (USA)
Venue: Astrodome, Houston, Texas
Result: Ali won by unanimous decision (12th round)

Fight 35: December 26, 1971
Opponent: Juergen Blin (Germany)
Venue: Hallenstadion, Zurich, Switzerland
Result: Ali won by knockout (7th round)

Fight 36: April 1, 1972
Opponent: McArthur Foster (USA)
Venue: Nippon Budokan, Tokyo, Japan
Result: Ali won by unanimous decision (15th round)

Fight 37: May 1, 1972
Opponent: George Chuvalo (Canada)
Venue: Pacific Coliseum, Vancouver, Canada
Result: Ali won by unanimous decision (12th round)

Fight 38: June 27, 1972
Opponent: Jerry Quarry (USA)
Venue: Convention Center, Las Vegas, Nevada
Result: Ali won by technical knockout (7th round)

Fight 39: July 19, 1972
Opponent: Alvin Lewis (USA)
Venue: Croke Park, Dublin, Republic of Ireland
Result: Ali won by technical knockout (11th round)

Fight 40: September 20, 1972
Opponent: Floyd Patterson (USA)
Venue: Madison Square Garden, New York City, New York
Result: Ali won when Patterson retired (7th round)

Fight 41: November 21, 1972
Opponent: Bob Foster (USA)
Venue: Sahara Tahoe Hotel, Stateline, Nevada
Result: Ali won by knockout (8th round)

Fight 42: February 14, 1973
Opponent: Joe Bugner (Hungary/UK/Australia)
Venue: Convention Center, Las Vegas, Nevada
Result: Ali won by unanimous decision (12th round)

Fight 43: March 31, 1973
Opponent: Ken Norton (USA)
Venue: Sports Arena, San Diego, California
Result: Ali lost by split decision (12th round)

Fight 44: September 10, 1973
Opponent: Ken Norton (USA)
Venue: Forum, Inglewood, California
Result: Ali won by split decision (12th round)

Fight 45: October 20, 1973
Opponent: Rudi Lubbers (the Netherlands)
Venue: Bung Karno Stadium, Jakarta, Indonesia
Result: Ali won by unanimous decision (12th round)

Fight 46: January 28, 1974
Opponent: Joe Frazier (USA)
Venue: Madison Square Garden, New York City, New York
Result: Ali won by unanimous decision (12th round)

Fight 47: October 30, 1974
Opponent: George Foreman (USA)
Venue: Stade de 20 Mai, Kinshasa, Zaire (Democratic Republic of the Congo)
Result: Ali won by knockout (8th round)

Fight 48: March 24, 1975
Opponent: Chuck Wepner (USA)
Venue: Richfield Coliseum, Richfield, Ohio
Result: Ali won by technical knockout (15th round)

Fight 49: May 16, 1975
Opponent: Ron Lyle (USA)
Venue: Convention Center, Las Vegas, Nevada
Result: Ali won by technical knockout (11th round)

Fight 50: June 30, 1975
Opponent: Joe Bugner (Hungary/UK/Australia)
Venue: Merdeka Stadium, Kuala Lumpur, Malaysia
Result: Ali won by unanimous decision (15th round)

Fight 51: October 1, 1975
Opponent: Joe Frazier (USA)
Venue: Araneta Coliseum, Manila, the Philippines
Result: Ali won when Frazier retired (14th round)

Fight 52: February 20, 1976
Opponent: Jean-Pierre Coopman (Belgium)
Venue: Coliseo Roberto Clemente, San Juan, Puerto Rico
Result: Ali won by knockout (5th round)

Fight 53: April 30, 1976
Opponent: Jimmy Young (USA)
Venue: Capitol Center, Landover, Maryland
Result: Ali won by unanimous decision (15th round)

Fight 54: May 24, 1976
Opponent: Richard Dunn (UK)
Venue: Olympiahalle, Munich, Germany
Result: Ali won by technical knockout (5th round)

Fight 55: September 28, 1976
Opponent: Ken Norton (USA)
Venue: Yankee Stadium, New York City, New York
Result: Ali won by unanimous decision (15th round)

Fight 56: May 16, 1977
Opponent: Alfredo Evangelista (Uruguay)
Venue: Capitol Center, Landover, Maryland
Result: Ali won by unanimous decision (15th round)

Fight 57: September 29, 1977
Opponent: Earnie Shavers (USA)
Venue: Madison Square Garden, New York City, New York
Result: Ali won by unanimous decision (15th round)

Fight 58: February 15, 1978
Opponent: Leon Spinks (USA)
Venue: Hilton Hotel, Las Vegas, Nevada
Result: Ali lost by split decision (15th round)

Fight 59: September 15, 1978
Opponent: Leon Spinks (USA)
Venue: Superdome, New Orleans, Louisiana
Result: Ali won by unanimous decision (15th round)

Fight 60: October 2, 1980
Opponent: Larry Holmes (USA)
Venue: Caesars Palace, Las Vegas, Nevada
Result: Ali lost after retiring (10th round)

Fight 61: December 11, 1981
Opponent: Trevor Berbick (Jamaica/Canada)
Venue: Queen Elizabeth Sports Centre, Nassau, the Bahamas
Result: Ali lost by unanimous decision (10th round)

QUOTABLE ALI

Muhammad Ali's quick wit and way with words livened up many press conferences and interviews, both during his boxing career and in his retirement. Here is just a small selection of quotes from the man nicknamed the "Louisville Lip."

"**YES THE CROWD DID NOT DREAM** WHEN THEY LAID DOWN THEIR MONEY, THAT THEY WOULD SEE A **TOTAL ECLIPSE OF THE SONNY**."
– During a press conference before his 1964 fight with Sonny Liston

"**STAY IN COLLEGE**, GET THE **KNOWLEDGE**... IF THEY CAN MAKE **PENICILLIN OUT OF MOLDY BREAD**, THEY CAN SURE MAKE **SOMETHING OF YOU!**"
– To a college audience during his lecture tour in the late 1960s

"I'M **NOT FIGHTING ONE MAN**. I'M **FIGHTING A LOT OF MEN**, SHOWING A LOT OF 'EM, **HERE IS ONE MAN THEY COULDN'T DEFEAT**, COULDN'T CONQUER. MY MISSION IS TO BRING **FREEDOM TO 30 MILLION BLACK PEOPLE**."
– During his exile from boxing for his stand on the Vietnam War

FLOAT LIKE A BUTTERFLY, STING LIKE A BEE. HIS **HANDS CAN'T HIT** WHAT HIS EYES CAN'T SEE.

– Before the 1964 fight against Sonny Liston

WHAT I SUFFERED PHYSICALLY WAS WORTH WHAT **I'VE ACCOMPLISHED IN LIFE.** A MAN WHO IS NOT **COURAGEOUS ENOUGH TO TAKE RISKS** WILL NEVER ACCOMPLISH ANYTHING IN LIFE.

– At a news conference in Houston, in 1984

I'M **SO FAST** THAT **LAST NIGHT** I TURNED OFF THE LIGHT IN MY **HOTEL ROOM** AND **GOT INTO BED BEFORE** THE **ROOM WAS DARK!**

– At a press conference before his fight against George Foreman in 1974

I WON'T MISS BOXING. **BOXING WILL MISS ME.**

– On his retirement, in 1981

THE **MAN WHO VIEWS THE WORLD** AT 50 THE SAME AS HE DID **AT 20** HAS **WASTED 30 YEARS** OF HIS LIFE.

– In an interview for a lifestyle and entertainment magazine, in 1975

I GUESS **I'D SETTLE** FOR BEING **REMEMBERED ONLY AS A GREAT BOXER** WHO BECAME A LEADER AND **CHAMPION OF HIS PEOPLE**. AND I **WOULDN'T EVEN MIND** IF FOLKS **FORGOT HOW PRETTY I WAS**.

– In his autobiography The Soul Of A Butterfly, *published in 2004*

ALI TRIVIA

Do you know everything about "The Greatest"? Check out this collection of surprising and lesser-known facts about Muhammad Ali, a man of many talents.

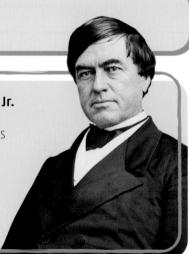

Cassius Marcellus Clay Jr. was named after his father, who himself was **named after a white American plantation owner** (pictured) from the 19th Century who campaigned for the **abolition of slavery**.

As a child obsessed with boxing, Cassius got his brother, Rudy, to **throw stones and rocks at him** so he could practice his **ducking and weaving** to dodge them.

In 1961, Cassius Clay **played a hoax on a news reporter** and photographer telling them that he **trained underwater** in a swimming pool. A **photo feature** showing his unusual training method was **published in *Life* magazine** and **fooled** everyone.

The **gloves Muhammad Ali wore** in 1965 when he **defeated Floyd Patterson** were sold in 2014 at a charity auction **for $1.1 million**. The winning bidder was the CEO of the Ultimate Fighting Championship, a mixed martial arts company.

In 1969, Ali **was paid a large sum** (believed to be $900,000) **to lend his support** to a new chain of **fast food restaurants** called Champburger that had opened in Miami.

Ali and former heavyweight champion **Rocky Marciano** took part in a mock bout called **"The Super Fight,"** which was shown in hundreds of **movie theaters in 1970**. The pair filmed scenes where they pretended to box each other, even acting out different endings to the fight with the eventual result chosen by a computer. In North America, the **ending saw Marciano win**, but in Europe, a different result saw **Ali knock Marciano out**.

Ali was **a huge fan of magic** and would often perform **disappearing coin and handkerchief tricks** to entertain people of all ages.

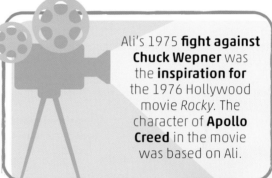

Ali's 1975 **fight against Chuck Wepner** was the **inspiration for** the 1976 Hollywood movie *Rocky*. The character of **Apollo Creed** in the movie was based on Ali.

In 1975, HBO became the first television network to **continuously deliver a broadcast of a sports event by satellite** when it showed the **"Thrilla in Manila"** bout between Ali and Joe Frazier. This was also the **first pay-per-view fight** to be made available to American households.

The American publisher **DC Comics** produced a new 72-page superhero comic called *Superman vs. Muhammad Ali* in 1978. In the comic, **Ali teams up with Superman** to defeat an alien invasion of Earth.

GLOSSARY

amateur
A person who takes part in a sport but is not paid for it.

apartheid
A political policy that involves keeping people of different racial groups apart in their daily lives. This was government policy in South Africa between 1948–1991. People who opposed it were part of the anti-apartheid movement.

assassinate
To murder someone, often a significant figure, and usually for political or religious reasons.

bout
Another word for a competitive fight between two boxers.

boxing commission
An organization that runs boxing in a region or an entire country.

boxing promoter
A person who sets up and promotes boxing fights as well as events featuring different boxers.

boycott
A way of protesting in which people refuse to use a service, take part in an event or activity, or buy a particular product.

civil rights
The rights that every person should have regardless of his or her sex, race, or religion. In the United States, the Civil Rights Movement sought to secure equal civil rights for African-Americans.

communism
A political theory and system in which the government owns the country's wealth and property and shares them with its citizens.

conscientious objector
A person who refuses to serve in the military or fight in wars due to his or her religious or moral beliefs.

cornerman
A cornerman is a coach or other member of a boxer's team who stands in the corner of the ring and tends their boxer in between rounds.

draft (military use)
A system in the United States during wartime that requires young men to join the armed forces for a period of service.

entourage
A group of people that accompany and look after an important or famous person.

exhibition bout
A boxing contest that is not fought for a title and where the result is not counted in a boxer's official record of wins and losses.

heavyweight
The heaviest of the major weight divisions in boxing. Male boxers in this division weigh more than 198 lb (90 kg), while female boxers weigh more than 175 lb (79 kg).

hook
A type of powerful punch thrown by a boxer in a curving arc by swinging his or her arm.

jab
A quick punch that starts from just under the fighter's chin. It is the most common type of punch used in boxing.

knockout
The early end of a fight when a boxer is knocked down by his opponent, and cannot get up to be ready to continue after the referee's count of 10 seconds.

license (boxing)
A document or list of documents that grant a person the right to take part in competitive boxing. People seeking a boxing license often have to submit details of their boxing experience and undergo a physical examination.

light-heavyweight
A weight division in boxing between super-middleweight and heavyweight. Male boxers in this division weigh between 175 lb (79 kg) and 200 lb (91 kg), while female boxers weigh between 168 lb (76 kg) and 175 lb (79 kg).

marine
The name given to a member of the United States Marine Corps, a branch of the country's armed forces.

Mixed Martial Arts (MMA)
A combat sport in which the contestants use a combination of fighting techniques from boxing, wrestling, and martial arts such as judo and kickboxing.

motorcade
A procession, usually of slow-moving cars or other motor vehicles traveling together.

non-violence
A type of protest where people do not damage property or harm others. Non-violent protests include peaceful marches and refusing to buy a company's goods or use its services.

Parkinson's disease
A disease caused by the loss of nerve cells in a specific part of the brain, which affects mobility and control of the body.

patriotism
To show support and great pride in one's country.

physique
The size, shape, and overall appearance of a person's body.

professional
A person who takes part in a sport as a job and is paid to participate.

racism
The belief that all members of a particular race possess similar qualities and abilities, and that they are superior or inferior to other races.

sabotage
To deliberately damage or destroy property, or hamper the progress of others. In wartime, this can include the damaging or destruction of bridges, airfields, or other facilities.

segregation
The deliberate separation of two things or people. Racial segregation is the forced separation in daily life of two or more sets of people based on their race or ethnic group.

slavery
A social system in which a certain section of people are owned, bought, and sold like property. Referred to as slaves, these people are made to work without wages.

sparring
A form of training where a boxer practices his or her movements, punches, and defense tactics against another boxer, while usually wearing padded protective gear.

split decision
The term used to describe the result of a fight in which the judges are divided over the winner of the bout.

super-middleweight
A weight division in boxing between middleweight and light heavyweight. Male boxers in this division weigh between 168 lb (76 kg) and 175 lb (79 kg), while female boxers weigh between 160 lb (73 kg) and 168 lb (76 kg).

Supreme Court
The highest national law court in the United States.

technical knockout
The stopping of a boxing bout before all its rounds have been completed. This occurs mostly due to the referee believing that one boxer cannot defend himself or herself properly or has suffered a serious injury.

unanimous decision
The term used to describe the result of a fight in which all judges agree unanimously on the winner at the end of a fight.

underdog
A contender in a sport who is thought to have a lesser chance of winning than the favorite.

weigh-in
The weighing of each boxer shortly before a fight to ensure that he or she is within the weight limits of the division.

welterweight
A weight division in boxing between lightweight and middleweight. Male boxers in this division weigh between 147 lb (67 kg) and 154 lb (70 kg), while female boxers weigh between 140 lb (64 kg) and 147 lb (67 kg).

INDEX

ACKNOWLEDGMENTS

Dorling Kindersley would like to thank the following people for their assistance with this book:
Priyanka Kharbanda for editorial assistance, Mohammad Rizwan for technical assistance, Caroline Stamps for proofreading, and Elizabeth Wise for the index.

Picture Credits

The publisher would like to thank the following for their kind permission to reproduce their photographs:

(Key: a-above; b-below/bottom; c-center; f-far; l-left; r-right; t-top)

2 Getty Images: Bettmann. **3 Getty Images:** The Stanley Weston Archive. **4 Getty Images:** Bettmann (ca, cra); The Stanley Weston Archive (cla); Steve Schapiro (bl); Popperfoto (br). **5 Getty Images:** Paula Bronstein / UNICEF (ca); R. McPhedran / Daily Express / Hulton Archive (cra). **Magnum Photos:** A. Abbas (cla). **Rex Shutterstock:** HeritageAuctions / Bournemouth News (br). **6–7 Getty Images:** The Stanley Weston Archive. **8 Bridgeman Images:** Christie's Images. **9 Getty Images:** Neil Leifer. **10–11 Getty Images:** Steve Schapiro. **12–13 Getty Images:** Universal History Archive. **12 Getty Images:** Buyenlarge (bl). **14–15 Getty Images:** Steve Schapiro. **16 Getty Images:** Bettmann. **17 USA TODAY Sports:** Tom Easterling / The Courier-Journal. **18–19 Getty Images:** New York Daily News Archive. **20–21 Getty Images:** Bettmann. **21 Getty Images:** CBS Photo Archive (ca). **22–23 Getty Images:** Jerry Cooke / Sports Illustrated. **24–25 Getty Images:** Bettmann. **26–27 Getty Images:** James Drake / The LIFE Images Collection. **28–29 USA TODAY Sports:** Warren Klosterman / The Courier-Journal. **30–31 Alamy Stock Photo:** Keystone Pictures USA. **32–33 Getty Images:** Chris Smith / Popperfoto. **34–35 Getty Images:** Art Rogers / Los Angeles Times. **35 Getty Images:** Underwood Archives (tr). **36–37 Getty Images:** Bettmann. **38–39 Getty Images:** Len Trievnor / Express. **39 Getty Images:** Bettmann (tr). **40–41 Getty Images:** Bettmann. **42 Getty Images:** Paul Slade / Paris Match. **43 Getty Images:** Bettmann. **44–45 Getty Images:** Tony Triolo / Sports Illustrated. **46 Getty Images:** James Drake / The LIFE Images Collection. **47 Getty Images:**

Richard Meek / Sports Illustrated. **48–49 Getty Images:** Bettmann. **50 Magnum Photos:** Thomas Hoepker. **51 Getty Images:** Bob Gomel / The LIFE Images Collection. **52–53 Magnum Photos:** Thomas Hoepker. **54–55 Getty Images:** Bettmann. **56–57 Getty Images:** Neil Leifer. **58–59 Alamy Stock Photo:** Everett Collection Historical. **60–61 Getty Images:** Bettmann. **61 Getty Images:** A. Y. Owen / The LIFE Images Collection (ca). **62–63 Alamy Stock Photo:** ZUMA Press, Inc.. **64–65 Getty Images:** Popperfoto. **65 Getty Images:** Joe Farrington / New York Daily News Archive (bc). **66 Getty Images:** Wally McNamee. **67 Getty Images:** CNP. **68–69 Getty Images:** Bettmann. **70–71 Getty Images:** Paul Slade / Paris Match. **71 Getty Images:** The Ring Magazine (ca). **72–73 Magnum Photos:** A. Abbas. **74–75 Getty Images:** Bettmann. **76–77 Alamy Stock Photo:** Keystone Pictures USA. **78–79 Getty Images:** The Ring Magazine. **79 Getty Images:** Larry Shaw / Shaw Family Archives (bl). **80–81 Getty Images:** Neil Leifer. **82–83 Getty Images:** Paul Slade / Paris Match. **84 Getty Images:** The Ring Magazine. **85 Getty Images:** Chris Smith / Popperfoto. **86–87 Alamy Stock Photo:** Everett Collection Inc. **86 Getty Images:** Tony Triolo / Sports Illustrated (bl). **88–89 Rex Shutterstock:** AP. **90–91 Getty Images:** Bettmann. **92–93 Getty Images:** Lawrence Schiller / Polaris Communications. **94 Getty Images:** Derek Hudson. **95 Getty Images:** Takeo Tanuma / Sports Illustrated. **96–97 Getty**

Images: Neil Leifer. **98–99 Getty Images:** John Iacono / Sports Illustrated. **100–101 Getty Images:** Paula Bronstein / UNICEF. **102–103 Getty Images:** Maria Bastone / AFP. **104–105 Getty Images:** Douglas Graham / Roll Call. **106–107 Getty Images:** Neil Leifer. **108 Getty Images:** Ray McManus / Sportsfile. **109 Getty Images:** Michael Cooper / Allsport. **110 Getty Images:** J. Michael Okoniewski / Liaison Agency. **111 Getty Images:** Chuck Kennedy / MCT / TNS. **112 Getty Images:** Mark Cornelison / Lexington Herald-Leader / TNS. **113 Getty Images:** VIEWpress. **114–115 Getty Images:** R. McPhedran / Daily Express / Hulton Archive. **116 Getty Images:** Bettmann (tr); Jerry Cooke / Sports Illustrated (bl). **117 Alamy Stock Photo:** Allstar Picture Library (bc). **Getty Images:** Volkan Furuncu / Anadolu Agency (crb); The Ring Magazine (tl); James Leynse (tr); Time & Life Pictures (clb). **119 Getty Images:** Bettmann. **120 Getty Images:** Bob Gomel / The LIFE Images Collection. **122 Library of Congress, Washington, D.C.:** LC-DIG-cwpbh-02748 (ca). **Rex Shutterstock:** HeritageAuctions / Bournemouth News (bl). **123 Alamy Stock Photo:** Lewton Cole (br); dpa picture alliance (cl). **Getty Images:** Bettmann (tr). **128 Getty Images:** Chris J Ratcliffe

All other images © Dorling Kindersley

For further information see:
www.dkimages.com

Ali's split glove from his 1963 bout against Henry Cooper